The Perfect Assassin: Lee Harvey Oswald, The CIA and Mind Control

A Unifying Hypothesis of the JFK Assassination

by
Jerry Leonard

© 2002 Jerry Leonard. All rights reserved.

No part of this book may be reproduced, stored in a retrieval system, or transmitted by any means, electronic, mechanical, photocopying, recording, or otherwise, without written permission from the author.

ISBN: 1-4033-6335-8 (e-book)
ISBN: 1-4033-6336-6 (Paperback)

This book is printed on acid free paper.

1stBooks – rev. 09/26/02

The Perfect Assassin

...I believe that one of the greatest dangers to modern society is the possible resurgence and expansion of the ideas of thought control...I think that one of the greatest dangers is that this shall increase until it encompasses all of the world.

-Richard Feynman (1965 Nobel Laureate, Physics)

Preface

After reading this book, you will find there is no "smoking gun," no single fact or piece of evidence anyone can point to as unequivocal proof of the scenario proposed. What I offer instead is a new way of looking at the JFK assassination, a theory I cannot conclusively prove any more than proponents of other theories of what really happened on that fateful day can prove theirs.

Due to its nature, much of what I report here is circumstance and supposition in an attempt to put together a 50-year puzzle that may forever have many of the pieces missing. As you go through this, I ask that you not jump to conclusions or hastily dismiss my body of evidence as too far-fetched.

In making my case, I present numerous eye-opening precedents which bolster the theory proposed while taking the reader through the years of Oswald's life leading up to November 1963, as well as the CIA activities at the time that would come to bear on the events discussed here.

I invite the JFK assassination research community to examine the model proposed herein—that mind-control can explain the inconsistencies in the assassination investigation—and gather and analyze data to determine whether the model is explanatory and predictive and then reject or accept the hypothesis as an explanation of the crime *based on the evidence*.

I ask you to be patient as I present my case and lay out my findings. And then when you finish, think back on what I have written. And ask yourself, "Is this not possible?"

Introduction

The successful use of hypnosis along the lines indicated in this memorandum would represent a serious threat to democratic values in times of peace and war. In addition, it might contribute to the development of unconventional methods of warfare, which will be widely regarded as immoral. The results of scientific research in the field under discussion would obviously lend themselves to offensive as well as defensive applications and to abuse no less than to use.[1]

- Irving L. Janis, 1949, U.S. Air Force, Project Rand Research Memorandum

Many elaborate conspiracy theories have been proposed to explain the assassination of President John F. Kennedy. Several attempt to exonerate the man the "establishment" accused of pulling the trigger—Lee Harvey Oswald—from any involvement in the assassination. These proponents typically portray Oswald as "just a patsy" set up to take the fall for either the Mafia, the CIA or both working in conjunction as they did against Cuba's leader Fidel Castro.[2]

On the other hand, many researchers (including the Warren Commission and the establishment press) have rejected conspiratorial plots and insist Oswald was the only assassin, a position rejected as the "lone nut" theory by its detractors.[3]

Notice the striking polarization in these two main themes. Either Oswald is completely left out of the picture, or he is the only one in it.

Consider instead a unifying "conspiracy" theory: that there was a CIA-backed plot to assassinate the president and that Oswald was the one who pulled the trigger. Further, this theory will propose that while Oswald was the assassin, he was an innocent patsy as well. These seemingly contradictory allegations can be harmonized by asserting that Oswald was a victim of the CIA's secret program to train "involuntary" assassins to do its bidding through advanced mind control technology, a technology that made headlines in the New York Times[4] decades after it had most likely been perfected.[5]

This theory provides a singular framework for unifying the pro- and anti-conspiracy theories and, as such, puts a new perspective on the Kennedy assassination, an event that nearly 40 years later continues to captivate and divide thoughtful members of the American public.

Part One

Have we the nerve and the will? Can we carry through in an age when we will witness not only new breakthroughs in weapons of destruction, but also a race for mastery of the sky and the rain, the ocean and the tides, the far side of space, and the inside of men's minds? [6]

-John F. Kennedy, 1959

When John F. Kennedy was assassinated November 22, 1963, in Dallas, it took the police only a short time to arrest a former U.S. Marine and defector to the Soviet Union named Lee Harvey Oswald. Before Oswald could be brought to trial, he himself was slain on national television by Jack Ruby.

Oswald was known to have led an interesting life, joining the Marines at the age of 17, defecting to the Soviet Union, returning to the States with a Russian wife (whose uncle was in the Soviet intelligence network[7]) and subsequently participating in both pro and anti-Communist political activities. In fact, as many researchers have noted, Oswald seemed to have lived a double life, bouncing between the ideological rails of militant pro-Communism and rabid anti-Communism.[8]

Although this duality in his ideological predispositions and activities has puzzled many researchers, this pattern may actually explain much about who was ultimately responsible for the assassination of JFK. As such, it strongly suggests that Oswald was being used as an unwitting tool of the CIA and FBI.[9]

CIA Memo Foreshadows Kennedy Assassination

Declassified CIA documents reveal that the scenario of the assassination of a U.S. official by a defector followed by the elimination of the assassin while in police custody had been discussed as a potential intelligence operation nearly a decade prior to the infamous events in Dallas. This proposed assassination would be unique in that the killer would be a victim of CIA mind-control technology and would not necessarily be conscious of, or responsible for, what he was doing.[10]

News of such CIA research programs to create "programmed" assassins was released to the general public in a *New York Times* article on February 9, 1978. This article reported the following information regarding a long-running CIA program to train mind-controlled assassins:

> The Central Intelligence Agency began a study in 1954 to find out whether a person could be secretly induced to commit an assassination against his will, newly released Government documents disclosed today.[11]

The declassified record indicates that U.S. intelligence agencies considered using these <u>mind-control techniques (developed in programs code-named ARTICHOKE, MKDELTA and MKULTRA)</u> to kill political figures *including American officials*.

Detailed information about one such planned assassination (under the project code-named ARTICHOKE) was revealed in an edited 1950s-era CIA memorandum quoted in the *Times* article:

> "As a 'trigger mechanism,' for a bigger project, it was proposed that an individual, of (deleted) descent, approximately 35 years old, well educated, proficient in English and well established socially and politically in the (deleted) government *be induced under Artichoke to perform an act, involuntarily, against a prominent (deleted) politician or if necessary, against an American official.*"[12][emphasis added]

The CIA memorandum continued:

> "After the act of attempted assassination was performed, it was assumed that the subject would be taken into custody by the (deleted) government and thereby 'disposed of.'"

Consider the parallels between this *proposed* CIA-backed assassination and the events in Dallas: Oswald, a defector, after allegedly committing the assassination of a high-level American official, Kennedy, was "taken into custody" by agents of the American government in Dallas and shortly thereafter "disposed of" by Jack Ruby on national television in the basement of a Dallas city jail.

Although news of the CIA's assassin training program was released through the *New York Times* in the 1970s, it was not until 1993 (nearly 30 years after the publication of the Warren Commission Report) that a front page article in the *New York Times* would reveal that Oswald, the alleged "lone nut" responsible for the Kennedy assassination, had more incriminating ties to the CIA than we were originally led to believe.

On August 24, 1993, *The New York Times* revealed that Oswald had not only been associating with CIA assassins[13] prior to Kennedy's death but was under nearly constant surveillance by both the CIA and the FBI while doing it![14] These facts have enormous implications.

The decades of post-assassination investigative efforts have peeled away many levels of CIA disinformation designed to portray Oswald as a lone-nut assassin. These efforts have revealed numerous leads consistent with the thesis that Oswald was in fact connected with CIA operations ongoing at the time of the JFK assassination and that the CIA was fully aware of Oswald's activities leading up to the assassination. Many of these leads are also consistent with the hypothesis that CIA-backed mind-control techniques were used in the assassination.

It is the author's opinion that the evidence linking Oswald to mind control and the CIA can be more fully appreciated with a deeper understanding of the CIA's various mind-control programs and the uses to which the technologies developed within these programs might be put in the field of espionage.

An Overview of CIA Mind Control Experimentation

"War is the end of all law. When we speak of keeping within the rules of the game we are childish, because it is not a game and true rules never hold. In the last analysis any device is justifiable which enables us to protect ourselves from defeat."

-George Estabrooks, Military Hypnosis Expert

In order to induce a person to commit an assassination attempt against his will, the CIA conducted a major research and testing program on mind-control techniques that involved, among other things, the use of hypnosis, drugs and psychotherapy. This developmental program to create assassins was part of a massive and more general program designed to develop mind-control technology, as summarized in a *New York Times* article on August 2, 1977:

> Several prominent medical research institutions and Government hospitals in the United States and Canada were involved in a secret, 25-year, $25-million effort by the Central Intelligence Agency to learn how to control the human mind. ...It sought to crack the mental defenses of enemy agents—to be able to program them and its own operatives to carry out any mission even against their will and "against such fundamental laws of nature as self-preservation."[15]

The largest project in the government's vast mind-control program was called Project MKULTRA. A joint Congressional hearing in 1977 titled "Project MKULTRA, The CIA's Program Of Research In Behavioral Modification" revealed the scope of this project:

> MKULTRA was the principal CIA program involving the research and development of chemical and biological agents. It was "concerned with the research and development of chemical, biological, and radiological materials capable of employment in clandestine operations to control human behavior."

Elsewhere in the same investigation it was reported that an impressive array of academic and paramilitary disciplines was employed in a crash program designed to find every means available for controlling human behavior:

> Over the ten-year life of the program, many "additional avenues to the control of human behavior" were designated as appropriate for investigation under the MKULTRA charter. *These include "radiation, electroshock, various fields of psychology, psychiatry, sociology, and anthropology, graphology, harassment substances, and paramilitary devices and materials."*[16] [emphasis added]

The MKULTRA program included extensive research into the use of drugs in controlling the minds of human subjects. LSD was one of the major drugs used in this mind-control program, which eventually included many tests on an unsuspecting public (including hundreds of military personnel). As described in the joint Congressional hearing in 1977:

> LSD was one of the materials tested in the MKULTRA program. The final phase of LSD testing involved surreptitious administration to unwitting nonvolunteer subjects in normal life settings by undercover officers of the Bureau of Narcotics acting for the CIA.

A hint at how extensive this testing was could be found in the same study:

> *...the effectiveness of the substances on individuals at all social levels, high and low, native American and foreign, is of great significance and testing has been performed on a variety of individuals within these categories.* [emphasis added][17]

Although numerous studies[18] and articles in the popular press[19] have been published over the years on the subject of MKULTRA and related tests, the full extent of the testing conducted on unwitting American citizens is not known since the records of the experiments were allegedly destroyed by CIA personnel. We do know, however, that in the LSD experiments, tests were conducted on people in numerous locations including bars, houses of prostitution, hospitals (on patients as well as doctors, nurses and attendants) and other "life settings."[20] We also know that at least one of these tests resulted in the death of the unwitting participant—a high-level[21] government biological warfare researcher.[22] Researchers have tied other suspicious deaths to this mind-control program[23] that allowed the CIA to engage in criminal behavior not only with reckless abandon[24] but with high-level blessing.[25]

The *New York Times* reported that many mind-control experiments were actually conducted by the civilian medical establishment (while being secretly funded and coordinated by the CIA through a network of foundations) under the pretext of legitimate medical research.[26] The CIA was so effective at compartmentalizing and funding the research covertly through various "front" organizations that in many cases the doctors involved in different components of the research were not even aware that they were working for the CIA. For example, LSD research was originally conducted by psychologists because researchers thought its effects on people would provide them a model form of schizophrenia that could be induced at will in human subjects and studied in the lab under controlled conditions. (As it turned out, the "trip" induced by LSD was not the same as schizophrenia.) Likewise, hypnosis was used by the Soviets as a way to induce neuroses in experimental subjects so that they could observe its effects in the lab. (Researchers would tell subjects during a hypnotic trance that they had committed some abhorrent act and then, following the hypnosis session, watch to determine how the induced subconscious guilt affected the behavior of the unwitting subjects.[27] This technique was also allegedly used by the Soviets to induce subjects to make false confessions with respect to undesirable political behavior.[28])

Another example of "legitimate" medical research (openly published in the scientific literature) that could be conveniently used as a cover to further the brainwashing research goals of the CIA includes so-called "depatterning" research. A summary of the objectives of this type of research was published in an article in the *Archives of Neurology and Psychiatry* in 1950. In this article, scientists reported on their research, which involved psychological conditioning after the administration of drugs in clinical therapeutic settings to answer the following sweeping and profound questions:

> If the neural arrangements underlying reaction patterns are reversible, could an adult's patterns be erased by a physiological process which would attack these neural arrangements? In other words, *could an adult be made, theoretically, patternless—could he be returned to a state of neurological and psychologic infancy for a short period?* If he could, then *could the formulation of new patterns be promptly induced during this period*, when old patterns were absent? If new patterns were set up, would they be enduring? If affirmative answers to these questions could be given, or even approached, could the procedure be employed psychotherapeutically? *If so, one would have a means of altering behavior by working with some of its fundamental neural foundations*, and the most basic aspect of therapy would be on a physiological level.[29] [emphasis added]

If an individual could "be returned to a state of neurological and psychologic infancy" and then have "the formulation of new patterns...promptly induced during this period," the psychologists (and those that employed them) would have tremendous levers of control over individual behavior. To evaluate the feasibility of implementing such techniques, the CIA conducted numerous "depatterning" experiments on unsuspecting patients at universities and other medical institutions.

At the Allan Memorial Institute at McGill University in Montreal, patients who were voluntarily seeking treatment for mental illness were instead "depatterned" using techniques developed by a prominent researcher named Ewen Cameron. In these experiments they "were put into a drugged sleep for weeks or months, subjected to electroshock therapy until they were 'depatterned,' knowing neither who or where they were, and forced to listen repeatedly to recorded messages broadcast from speakers on the wall or under their pillows."[30]

In one case, a woman named Rita Zimmerman was given 30 sessions of electroshock treatment followed by 56 days of drug-induced sleep. Another woman named Linda Macdonald spent 86 days in the "sleep room" at McGill, was given 109 shock treatments and saturated with barbiturates and other drugs.[31] According to the *New York Times*, "When she got out of the experiment, she could not read or write, had to be toilet-trained and could not remember her husband, her five children or any part of the first 26 years of her life."[32] As one author who interviewed Linda summarized: "Not only did she not know her husband, she didn't even know what a husband was."[33] (In similar tests, prisoners at federal drug hospitals were used in LSD experiments that, in one example, included keeping seven men on LSD for 77 days in a row.[34] In other experiments, children were given LSD daily, for up to a year.[35])

As a result of the experiments at McGill,[36] the Canadian government granted damages of $80,000 to approximately 80 patients of this hospital. The U.S. government also granted damages to individuals who went in for voluntary treatment "and didn't realize until much later that they were being used in experiments."[37]

Lest the reader think that these treatments were administered by obscure quacks on the margins of the field of psychology, Dr. Cameron, the researcher who pioneered these techniques and oversaw their implementation at McGill, was named president of both the American and Canadian Psychiatric Associations, was chairman of the Canadian Scientific Planning Committee and was the first president of the World Association of Psychiatrists.[38] (He also had a U.S. security clearance.[39])

Likewise, the American doctors who did the research for the CIA's vast mind-control program were among the elite of their profession. Colin Ross wrote that the "interlocking academic relationships of the mind control doctors involved the most influential figures in American psychiatry in the second half of the twentieth century."[40] Continuing, Ross summarized:

> Contractors on CIA and military mind control research included leading psychiatrists and psychologists, Past Presidents and Awardees of the American Psychiatric Association, editors and associate editors of leading professional journals, Chairmen of academic Departments of Psychiatry, and their colleagues and coauthors.[41]

In addition to experiments with psychic driving and depatterning (some of which were published in the open literature), experiments were conducted by the medical community in which hypnosis and drugs were investigated for their effects on learning,[42] memory[43] and conditioning.[44] Experiments were also conducted that involved combining the administration of psychoactive drugs with hypnosis. For example, many drugs were investigated "as an aid in producing and deepening the hypnotic state in selected resistant patients."[45] (Electric shock therapy was investigated as a means of causing amnesia and amplifying the hypnotic state.)

Combining drugs and hypnosis provided other interesting benefits in addition to allowing scientists to hypnotize subjects who were not otherwise readily susceptible to hypnosis. By hypnotizing subjects while they were under the influence of certain drugs, doctors were able to use hypnosis to both neutralize the effects of the drugs as well as to artificially and spontaneously induce a drug "trip."[46] As the authors of one study summarized: "It was possible to make one subject normal by hypnosis at the height of her LSD-25 experience. Three weeks later, it was possible to reproduce an LSD psychedelic experience by hypnosis alone."[47, 48]

By compartmentalizing the behavior modification-oriented research grants and farming out the developmental work to numerous (and often unsuspecting) researchers, agencies and hospitals, the CIA was able to covertly run a vast mind-control research and testing effort under the pretext of legitimate medical research using the civilian health sciences infrastructure.[49] The *Washington Post* recently noted that the program covertly administered by CIA personnel included a vast network of psychological and medical experiments conducted in hospitals, universities, research labs, prisons and safe houses, many of them carried out on unsuspecting subjects—mental patients, prostitutes and their johns, drug addicts, and anyone else who stumbled into the CIA's web. Some had been subjected to electroshock therapy in an effort to alter their behavior. Some endured prolonged sensory deprivation. Some were doped and made to sleep for weeks in an attempt to induce an amnesia-like state. Others suffered a relentless loop of audiotape playing the same message hundreds of thousands of times.[50]

The extent of these experiments on "many thousands of prisoners and mental patients" prompted Ross to compare them with experiments conducted in the infamous Nazi concentration camps:

At Nuremberg, Nazi doctors who experimented with mescaline in the death camps were regarded as war criminals. A decade later, such research was conducted by the leading figures in academic psychiatry in North America, and published in the leading medical journals.[51]

Ross noted, "If such procedures were carried out under Third World dictators, they would be denounced as human rights violations by American and Canadian psychiatry, and would be called *brainwashing*."[52]

Espionage and Hypnosis

"...the key to creating an effective spy or assassin rests in splitting a man's personality, or creating multipersonality, with the aid of hypnotism...This is not science fiction. This has and is being done. I have done it."
-George Estabrooks

Hypnosis had unique and powerful applications in the field of espionage. Such applications included the training of couriers,[53] double agents and assassins.

Several fascinating aspects of hypnosis make it such a potent weapon for intelligence uses. One is the familiar use of post-hypnotic suggestion to manipulate people into performing acts against their will. Also, the induction of "selective amnesia" under hypnosis provides numerous advantages that can be exploited by intelligence agencies. (Although the exact mechanism underlying this attribute of hypnosis has been debated within the medical community[54] it is nevertheless a very real and powerful phenomenon.[55]) The capability of inducing selective amnesia allowed the possibility of eliminating potential security threats by selectively removing information from the memory of an agent or operative. An agent could be sent into the field to perform various tasks and, later, as a result of post-hypnotic suggestion, have no recollection of even being involved in these operations!

In addition to preventing agents from remembering that they had been used as operatives, the well-documented phenomenon of selective post-hypnotic amnesia promised many other fascinating benefits. The use of hypnosis could aid in the creation of more effective couriers since it would allow intelligence agencies to implant sensitive information into a subject's subconscious mind that could only be accessed under hypnosis by a "friendly" hypnotist.[56] Through the use of post-hypnotic suggestion and hypnotic amnesia, a courier used in a given operation would not only be unaware that he was carrying sensitive information[57] but would not even remember transferring the information to a friendly intelligence asset. Military hypnotist George Estabrooks, a Harvard-trained psychologist, summarized: "Given a good hypnotic subject to work with, we can deliver secret messages with perfect assurance that they will never be discovered."[58]

Did the U.S. government actually use these methods for creating couriers? Estabrooks claimed to have used it for military applications during World War II on an Army Service Corps Captain he named "Smith." As Estabrooks related in a 1971 article in *Science Digest*:

> The "hypnotic courier," on the other hand, provides a unique solution. I was involved in preparing many subjects for this work during World War II. The system is virtually foolproof. As exemplified by the case, the information literally was "locked" in Smith's unconscious for retrieval by the only two people who knew the combination. The subject had no conscious memory of what happened, so couldn't spill the beans. No one else could hypnotize him even if they might know the signal phrase.[59]

These experiments were apparently continued after the war. A declassified 1954 proposal from a mind-control doctor to the CIA published by Ross contained the following summary of the use and benefits of a hypnotic courier:

> The safeguarding of the messages entrusted to couriers. In deep hypnosis the subject, military or civilian, can be given a message to be delivered to say Colonel X in Berlin. The subject may then be sent to Berlin on any perfectly routine assignment. The message will be perfectly safe and will be delivered to the proper person because the subject will have no memory whatsoever in the waking state as to the nature and contents of the message. It can be arranged that the subject will have no knowledge of ever having been hypnotized. It can be arranged that no one beside Colonel X in Berlin can hypnotize the subject and recover the message. Secondly, if by any chance, he is picked up through leakage of information from any other sources the message is safe. No amount of third degree tactics can pry it loose, for he simply does not have it in his conscious mind. Even if the enemy suspects the use of hypnotism the message is still safe for no one can hypnotize him except this Colonel X in Berlin.[60]

As will be shown shortly, at the time this proposal was written, the CIA was conducting field trials on even more sophisticated uses of hypnosis in espionage.

It has also been alleged that, in addition to being useful for selectively inhibiting a person's memory, hypnosis can be used as a means of enhancing memory. This capability, known as hypermnesia,[61] would provide a valuable tool for couriers or spies and those that control them. Agents with this capability could be programmed to remember certain documents, people, geography or industrial sites and then be sent into the field under post-hypnotic suggestion, to return to the proper authorities at the appropriate time and report the relevant information. Ross summarized the usefulness of such agents:

> As well as being potential couriers...the subjects could function in effect as hypnotically controlled cameras. They

could enter a room or building, memorize materials quickly, leave the building, and then be amnesic for the entire episode. The memorized material could then be retrieved by a handler using a previously implanted code or signal, without the amnesia being disturbed.[62]

While it may sound fantastic at first, agents equipped only with photographic memories have made unparalleled contributions in crucial military intelligence operations. For example, a young female French citizen, named Jeannie Rousseau, after being recruited by the allies as a spy in occupied Europe, used her self-described photographic memory during World War II to produce what the *Washington Post* described as "one of the great intelligence documents of World War II."[63]

The Creation of Double Agents Through Hypnosis

In addition to the training of couriers, hypnosis had other interesting applications useful to those engaged in the art of espionage. More sophisticated applications of hypnosis provided the ability to train agents to be convincing double agents who could not be hypnotized by unfriendly hypnotists and who would be impervious to interrogation and torture if subjected to such measures after being captured by hostile forces.

Resistance to Hostile Interrogation

U.S. officials were extremely interested in determining whether hypnosis could be used to "immunize" American spies against hypnotic interrogation by enemy forces. As Seymour Fisher, the author of one U.S. Air Force study, noted: "In any event, it is important to recognize the possibility that a nation might take measures for the event of capture by its personnel so that hypnotic interrogation would be unsuitable."[64]

Fisher further noted: "Through posthypnotic suggestion, a subject can be taught to respond inappropriately whenever he is being used by another hypnotist."[65] Inappropriate behavior patterns with which agents might be "programmed" as a means of obtaining "resistance to interrogation" might include "appropriately timed amnesias," induced periods of prolonged sleep and bouts of irrational behavior.

Hypnosis might also be used to build up resistance to physical,[66] psychological and social deprivation notoriously used by enemy forces to facilitate interrogations. Fisher again: "By extensive training in autosuggestion, personnel would be capable of postponing and temporarily

The Perfect Assassin

alleviating such primary deprivation states as hunger, thirst and fatigue. Autosuggestive control over pain stimulation would also tend to weaken the vulnerability of captured personnel exposed to pain-inducing stimuli."[67]

Multiple Personalities

One method of creating double agents or "super spies" consisted of using hypnosis to create multiple personalities in an individual. These "alter" personalities could reside in the same person and, unbeknownst to the individual, perform separate roles and even live out separate lives. This technology could be used to create double agents who wouldn't know they were double agents.

Although it initially sounds far-fetched, the ability to induce multiple personality through hypnosis has been documented in the medical literature. Experiments were published in the open literature in which 32 secondary school children who, after being pre-screened for susceptibility to deep hypnosis, had secondary personalities induced by hypnosis.[68] The author of one particular study reported that he had induced up to 10 alter personalities in some children.[69]

Such multiple personalities or dissociated states in adults could be used in the manner described above to render spies immune to interrogation. Fisher noted: "[P]osthypnotic depersonalization and related dissociative states could be built into the subjects so that if they fall into enemy hands, they would no longer function as rational, integrated individuals."[70]

There are other uses for multiple personalities in the espionage game. In a little-known book first published in 1943, Estabrooks (who claimed to be extensively involved in military applications of hypnosis[71]) described in great detail how a double agent or "super spy" could be created using hypnotically induced multiple personalities. In his book, *Hypnotism*, Estabrooks explained the process by which *unwitting* double agents could be created using hypnosis in the fight against Communism:

> We start with an excellent subject, and he must be just that, one of those rare individuals who accepts and who carries through every suggestion without hesitation. ...Then we start to develop a case of multiple personality though the use of hypnotism. In his normal waking state, which we will call Personality A, or PA, *this individual will become a rabid communist.* He will join the party, follow the party line and make himself as objectionable as possible to the authorities. Note that he will be acting in good faith. *He is a*

> *communist, or rather his PA is a communist and will behave as such.*[72] [emphasis added]

Estabrooks went on to explain how after hypnotically inducing a pro-Communist personality, a secondary anti-Communist personality could be created in the same individual:

> Then we develop Personality B (PB), the secondary personality, the unconscious personality, if you wish, although this is somewhat of a contradiction in terms. *This personality is rabidly American and anti-communist.* It has all the information possessed by PA, the normal personality, whereas PA does not have this advantage. [emphasis added]

He next explained how, together, these two artificially created personalities (one pro-Communist, one anti-Communist) could be used in harmony by the intelligence community for fascinating anti-Communist espionage purposes:

> My super spy plays his role as a communist in his waking state, aggressively, consistently, fearlessly. But his PB is a loyal American, and PB has all the memories of PA. As a loyal American, he will not hesitate to divulge those memories, and needless to say we will make sure he has the opportunity to do so when occasion demands.[73]

Estabrooks then went on to summarize the utility of using hypnotically induced multiple personality for creating invulnerable double agents or super spies to infiltrate suspect organizations:

> Once again these people would have a great advantage over ordinary "informers." Convinced of their own innocence, they would play the fifth column role with the utmost sincerity, and as mentioned before this conviction of innocence would probably be their greatest protection. Again, if suspected, no one could obtain from them any useful information. Only a very few key people could throw them into the trance and, without this, any attempt to get information would be useless.

The Benefits of Double Agents

Needless to say, the benefits to an intelligence agency derived from using double agents could be enormous. Double agents could provide valuable information to state intelligence agencies by infiltrating enemy institutions and informing on them—providing valuable inside information.

Double agents could also be employed to join *existing* groups, attain leadership positions and then recommend disastrous actions intended to divide, disrupt and discredit the group.[74] Discrediting the group might also serve the function of rationalizing government action against the targeted group or its stated goals.

A similar, though more sophisticated, form of this tactic could be used in which double agents would *create* groups that appeared to be sympathetic to an enemy government and use these institutions to keep track of enemy sympathizers who might join or interact with such groups. The benefits of this latter tactic were alluded to by Umberto Eco in his fictional work *Foucault's Pendulum*:

> …if you want to confound your enemies, the best technique is to create clandestine sects, wait for dangerous enthusiasms to precipitate, then arrest them all. *In other words, if you fear a plot, organize one yourself; that way, all those who join it come under your control.*[75] [emphasis added]

By infiltrating or forming allegedly pro-Communist organizations, anti-Communist agencies such as the FBI or CIA would have the opportunity to identify, track and control "leftists" who joined the organizations. These fake Communist "fronts" could then be used for discrediting political movements in the eyes of the public[76] or even serve as vehicles for tracking and/or influencing sympathetic foreign communist governments.

It would appear that prominent Communist and Socialist political groups in the U.S. frequently serve this intelligence function. The use of domestic groups in this manner have yielded much fruit for the intelligence agencies. A 1995 *New York Times* article[77] revealed that the FBI had long ago infiltrated "the highest circles of the American Communist Party" with several informants who were recruited in the early 1950s. The *Times* article notes that, according to a senior government official, these high-level informers were also a "treasure trove of information about the Soviet Union."[78]

Earlier reports in the *New York Times* revealed that the FBI, in addition to infiltrating the Communist Party, has thoroughly infiltrated the leadership of other domestic left-leaning political groups such as the Socialist Workers Party and the Young Socialist Alliance. In addition to having used 316 informers against the party (which, amazingly, represents more than 10 percent of its active membership of only 2,500), it was reported that at least 42 of these informants held leadership positions within the organizations.[79]

It should be obvious that if double agents were useful to intelligence agencies, double agents who were capable of carrying out their roles with genuine sincerity and without realizing they were being used would be even more valuable. To reiterate Estabrooks' statement on the advantages of such agents: "Convinced of their own innocence, they would play the fifth column role with the utmost sincerity, and ...this conviction of innocence would probably be their greatest protection." Estabrooks went on to note in another publication that if enemy intelligence groups "should suspect our man, and confront him with an accusation, he will be the very model of righteousness outraged." He continued, "He could not tell the truth about his life as a spy because he would not know it."[80]

While the extent of CIA use of these techniques is not known, Estabrooks claims to have used them extensively in military applications as early as WWII. Ross published a declassified 1954 proposal to the CIA from a would-be mind-control doctor. In this document, the author (who Ross identified as Estabrooks) proposed:

> A specific counterintelligence technique to be used against enemy agents....I will take a number of men and will establish in them through the use of hypnotism the condition of split personality. Consciously they will be ardent Communists, phanatical [sic] adherence to the party line, ready and eager to submit to any discipline which the party may prescribe. Unconsciously they will be loyal American just as grimley [sic] determined to thwart the Communists at every turn in the road.

The author continued:

> Consciously they will associate with the Communists and learn all the plans of the organization. Once every month or at such time is advisable, they will be contacted by a member of our intelligence department, hypnotized, and as

loyal Americans will tell what they know. This sounds unbelievable, but I assure you, it will work.[81]

Whatever the veracity of Estabrooks' claims, it is known that the CIA was at least conducting field trials using the hypnotic double agent in the 1950s. Ross published an internal CIA memo written in response to the above proposal and dated July 15, 1954. This memo, addressed "to the Chief, Security Research Staff from Chief, Technical Branch," contained the following passage:

> ...proposal about using hypnotized individuals as counteragents is also not new and we, of course, have discussed this many times. Whether or not it can in fact be demonstrated we are not sure and it's hoped that *the field tests we are working on may help us along these lines.* [emphasis added]

The argument will be made shortly that Lee Harvey Oswald himself was used as a double agent by the CIA to create, infiltrate, track and discredit Communist groups and indeed that he was prepared for this role (and his role as an assassin) through mind control.

The Creation of Assassins Through Hypnosis

> *Is hypnosis dangerous? It can be. Under certain circumstances, it is dangerous in the extreme. It has even been known to lead to murder. Given the right combination of hypnotist and subject, hypnosis can be a lethal weapon.*[82]
> -George Estabrooks

In addition to creating couriers and double agents through hypnosis, it is now well documented that the CIA was also very interested in creating mind-controlled assassins using this same technology.[83]

Although it has been vigorously denied by many hypnosis experts that a subject under hypnotic influence can be induced to commit a crime against his/her will while in a trance,[84,85] there are numerous documented cases in which anti-social acts have been committed under hypnosis in both laboratory[86] and real-life conditions.[87] The key to eliciting this type of behavior appears to be to alter the subject's perception while under trance *so that the anti-social act he is to be manipulated into committing does not appear to be anti-social* and therefore does not appear to violate his personal moral code. As described by one researcher:

> ...it is not difficult to induce anti-social behavior in a subject when his altered perception of reality does not allow for an awareness or identification of "anti-social" with the act he is actually performing.[88]

Estabrooks made similar observations about the ease with which skilled hypnotists could induce anti-social behavior:

> ...no reports of failures have yet been made in experiments of a more subtle type, where the hypnotist takes great care so to alter his subject's perception of the situation as to create in him the conviction that the required act is, rather than antisocial, actually desirable. The most compliant hypnotic subject may, for any number of reasons, resist a direct suggestion to steal. But if he is convinced that he is not stealing someone else's property, but recovering his own, he will commit acts of theft. *With the proper manipulation of his perceptions, he will do far worse things than that.*[89][emphasis added]

One method of altering the subject's perception is to convince him while under hypnosis that the desired anti-social act is necessary for a greater good or that he is in a mortal struggle of good-versus-evil (or for his own survival) that would require "extreme" forms of behavior.[90]

One example of the use of this technique to create anti-social behavior in experimental subjects was published in the *Journal of Abnormal and Social Psychology* shortly after World War II. In this experiment, U.S. soldiers were manipulated into aggressively attacking both superior officers and friends after having been told in a trance that the officer or friend was in fact an enemy Japanese soldier who was attempting to kill the subject.[91] (To the surprise of the researchers conducting one such experiment, the subject pulled a knife from his pocket and attempted to stab a friend and fellow officer posing as the enemy. Fortunately, the officer was able to deflect the thrust, and witnesses in the room alertly interceded to subdue the hypnotized subject.)

The Perfect Assassin

Did the CIA use such a technology to create programmed assassins? They certainly have investigated the possibility. An experiment in hypnosis along these lines was conducted by a researcher named Morse Allen who was intimately associated with the CIA mind-control program. This experiment was described by John Marks in his book *In Search of the Manchurian Candidate*. As Marks summarized:

> On February 19, 1954, Morse Allen simulated the ultimate experiment in hypnosis: the creation of a "Manchurian Candidate," or programmed assassin. Allen's "victim" was a secretary whom he put into a deep trance and told to keep sleeping until he ordered otherwise. He then hypnotized a second secretary and told her that if she could not wake up her friend, "her rage would be so great that she would not hesitate to 'kill.'" Allen left a pistol nearby, which the secretary had no way of knowing was unloaded. Even though she had earlier expressed a fear of firearms of any kind, she picked up the gun and "shot" her sleeping friend. *After Allen brought the "killer" out of her trance, she had apparent amnesia for the event, denying she would ever shoot anyone.*[92] [emphasis added]

Throughout the 1950s, the CIA wanted to try this powerful technology in "real life" experiments. As chronicled by Marks, the agency wanted to use hypnotic techniques *on a defector* to create an involuntary assassin:

> Early in 1954, Allen almost got his chance to try the crucial test. According to a CIA document, the subject was to be a 35-year-old, well-educated foreigner who had once worked for a friendly secret service, probably the CIA itself. He had now shifted his loyalty to another government, and the CIA was quite upset with him. *The Agency plan was to hypnotize him and program him into making an assassination attempt. He would then be arrested at the least for attempted murder and "thereby disposed of."* [emphasis added]

Marks claims that the proposed operation described above did not take place. However, according to Marks, Allen was given access to and allowed to continue experiments on other defectors and double agents using the CIA's mind-control technology designed to create programmed assassins.

Combinations

The techniques described above, which include the inducement of multiple personalities and the programming of assassins through hypnosis, while powerful in their own right, might be even more effective when used in combination. For example, an agent with an artificially split personality designed to enable the individual to work as a double agent might also have these separate personalities trained to engage in modes of anti-social behavior such as assassination.[93]

Assuming an operative had a pro and anti-Communist personality split along the lines described by Estabrooks, not only could the pro-Communist personality be used to infiltrate left wing organizations, but it might also be used as an ideologically motivated assassin against right wing political figures.[94]

Summary

Through the use of hypnosis and drugs, the CIA had an impressive arsenal of weapons that it might use to create mind-controlled spies and operatives. Government researchers openly claimed they not only could create spies and double agents using mind-control technology but that they actually had created them.[95] Does the mind-control technology described by well-connected researchers like Estabrooks[96] bear on the Kennedy assassination? The thesis that Oswald was indeed one victim of this powerful technology—trained to be a double agent as well as an involuntary assassin under the influence of drugs and hypnosis—will be explored below.[97] This theory ties together many previously inexplicable components of Oswald's troubled life.[98]

Jerry Leonard

Part Two

Jerry Leonard

Oswald's Double Life Explained?

Lee Harvey Oswald's many associations with characters and philosophies at opposite extremes of the geopolitical spectrum were elegantly summarized by author Bob Callahan:

> During the course of his very brief life, Lee Harvey Oswald was a street kid with mob connections in New Orleans; the up and coming President of his Junior High School class in the Bronx; a budding Marxist suspended from that class for refusing to salute the American flag; a patriotic Air Patrol Cadet in David Ferrie's private Air Force whose life's goal now was to join the Marines; a top secret Marine radar operator who worked on the U-2; a disenchanted Jarhead who spent his time spouting Marxist slogans to mysterious women companions in expensive Japanese bars; a young ONI agent who underwent language training in California preparatory to going underground in Russia; a Soviet defector treated like royalty by the Soviet officials, his uncle, his wife, and the KGB; a repatriated American welcomed with open arms by the neo-nazi White Russian community of Dallas, Texas; a reborn militant activist who openly proclaimed his support for Castro, while at the same time being secretly connected with one of the most vicious, anti-Castro paramilitary forces in the USA; and, finally, either the chief protagonist, or only a mere patsy, in the assassination of John Fitzgerald Kennedy.

Callahan went on to make the following observation:

> There appears to never have been one single Oswald. Rather, he seemed to preside over a number of different personalities, each one threatening to pull him apart at the seams. Psychologically speaking, Oswald does not appear to have been all that stable a fellow.[99]

This description of Oswald's polarized life is highly interesting in light of the limited knowledge we now have of CIA and military intelligence capabilities in the field of mind-control and, specifically, the creation and manipulation of multiple personalities with polarized political views for intelligence operations. In fact, the overview of Oswald's life provided by Callahan, in light of Estabrooks earlier writings, begs the question of whether Oswald's apparent psychological instability was enhanced or even induced using this mind-control technology.

In *The Search for the Manchurian Candidate*, Marks described how CIA psychiatrists could control behavior by inducing schizophrenia and creating multiple personalities under the influence of hypnosis:

> The hope was to take an existing ego state—such as an imaginary childhood playmate—and build it into a separate personality, unknown to the first. The hypnotist would communicate directly with this schizophrenic offshoot and command it to carry out specific deeds about which the main personality would know nothing...[100]

Perhaps this description of intentionally induced schizophrenia and multiple personalities could explain Oswald's contradictory ideological positions and his alleged psychological instability. If Oswald was indeed being psychologically manipulated as a double agent along the path explicitly described by Estabrooks,[101] then his *pro-Communist* personality could have been used to infiltrate Communist organizations as a means of monitoring them and their members or as a means of feeding these groups disinformation by *anti-Communist* intelligence agencies. As will be discussed shortly, evidence indicates that Oswald was used as an *agent provocateur*, a double agent used to infiltrate and discredit "enemy" organizations by engaging in illegal or undesirable behavior that could then be identified with the targeted group. Such programmed behavior modes could explain much of the mystery surrounding Oswald's life.

Oswald As Double Agent

The Defection to Russia
Over the years following the Kennedy assassination, there has been much speculation that Oswald's controversial defection to the Soviet Union was part of a planned U.S. intelligence operation and that he was merely "posing" as a leftist defector for intelligence reasons relating to a mission. What might have been the ultimate purpose of such an "arranged" defection?

Recall that Estabrooks, the Harvard hypnotist, outlined in the 1950s how multiple personalities might be induced in a subject to create a "super spy" who could infiltrate left wing organizations and gather intelligence on them:

> They would, as we said before, be urged in the waking state to become fifth columnist enemies to the United States, but we would also point out to them in hypnotism that this was really a pose, that their real loyalty lay with this country, offering them protection and reward for their activities. *Through them we would hope to be kept informed of the activities of their "friends,"* this information, of course, being obtained in the trance state. *They would also be very useful as "plants"* in concentration camps or *in any other situation where it was suspected their services might be of use to our intelligence department.* [emphasis added][102]

Was Oswald's defection to the Soviet Union as an alleged enemy of the United States part of such a premeditated plan by the U.S. intelligence agencies to gather information on the Soviet Union using a "plant" or human asset? Could many of Oswald's apparently hostile activities after leaving the Marines have been "in the waking state" as a simulated "fifth columnist" enemy of the United States?

John Newman, an assistant professor at the University of Maryland, raises many interesting questions relevant to this thesis in his intriguing 1995 book entitled *Oswald and the CIA*. Newman's research[103] reveals that, contrary to previous CIA testimony, Oswald was under nearly continuous surveillance by various U.S. intelligence organizations from the time of his defection to the Soviet Union up until the assassination of the president.[104]

Newman proposes, based on the anomalous manner in which Oswald's surveillance files were handled by U.S. intelligence agencies, that his defection to the Soviet Union was used in a highly sensitive counterintelligence operation designed to track down intelligence leaks to the Soviets.[105]

Newman postulates that Oswald's defection to the USSR was prearranged by the CIA as a "dangle" to determine whether there was a leak within the U.S. intelligence system regarding the super-secret American U-2 spy plane operations that flew over Russia and whether that leak was from a highly-placed Soviet "mole" in the U.S. The U.S. had received a warning from its own highly placed mole in the Soviet intelligence system (a Colonel Peter Semyonovich Popov) that the Soviets had obtained highly sensitive information on the U-2 operation *from someone within the U.S. system*.[106] By monitoring the way in which the Soviets treated Oswald's defection (due to his background as a Marine radar operator involved with monitoring U-2 flights from the Atsugi base in Japan), the U.S. should have been able to determine how much information the Soviets already had about the U-2 espionage capability[107] (which the U.S. had used against them with great success[108]).

There are numerous irregularities about Oswald's defection to Russia and return to the U.S. that are consistent with Newman's postulate that it was all a carefully staged and monitored episode. For example, the CIA seemed to handle Oswald's defection with marked indifference. Given the super-sensitive nature of the U-2 information Oswald supposedly had access to as a Marine (which he brazenly offered to give to the Soviets after his defection), a major damage assessment should have been conducted by the U.S. intelligence agencies to determine if their prized surveillance capability with the U-2 spy plane had been fatally compromised. But apparently no such assessment was undertaken. According to the official story, Oswald was not even debriefed by the CIA when he returned to the U.S. Nor was he prosecuted for offering to sell American military secrets to the Soviets. These suspicious facts were noted by Philip Melanson, an author and political science professor from Southeastern Massachusetts University:

> The Agency claims it had no interest in Oswald and never debriefed him upon his return from Russia. Was the CIA so simple-minded that it saw no possible connection between Oswald and the U-2? Did it see one but forget to follow up on it by debriefing him? Or did it already know precisely what Oswald had told the Soviets?[109]

Interestingly, in later conversations with co-workers, Oswald's discussion of his trip to the Soviet Union indicate that he was more aware of intelligence-related matters on his Russian odyssey than is commonly perceived. As Melanson summarized:

> Oswald proved himself to be a rather keen observer of the things around him. Back in Dallas a fellow worker remembers his commenting that the Soviet disbursement of military units was different from the U.S. pattern: the Soviets did not intermingle their armor and infantry

divisions, and they would have all of their aircraft in one location and all of their infantry in another.

Melanson then wryly noted: "These are curious interests for a befuddled young ideologue. With an eye for detail like that it is indeed a shame that the CIA missed talking to him."[110]

[There are several other peculiar facts surrounding Oswald's defection and the theory that this defection was related to the U-2 spy plane program. Curiously, the day Oswald reached Moscow, the high-level Russian intelligence agent who had warned of leaks involving the U-2 spy plane program was arrested by the Soviets. Also of interest, while Oswald was still in Russia, a U-2 pilot named Gary Powers was shot down over the USSR while on a reconnaissance mission. This mission over the Soviet Union was only the second flight over the USSR following Oswald's defection. Powers later blamed Oswald (who had been trained to track these planes as a radar technician at the Atsugi base in Japan) for providing the Soviets with enough information to track and destroy his plane.[111] In a final irony, following his re-defection to the U.S., Oswald the supposed Marxist would be employed by a Dallas graphic arts company that did classified work for the Army Map Service that used photos generated by spy planes such as the U-2.]

* * *

Did U.S. law enforcement and intelligence agencies really target the Soviets using lower-level U.S. military personnel *pretending* to be Soviet-friendly traitors? Are there any historical precedents for sophisticated operations resembling that proposed above to explain Oswald's "traitorous" pro-Soviet behavior? A recent exposé, entitled *Cassidy's Run: The Secret Spy War Over Nerve Gas*, by David Wise, provides an argument that, indeed, such high-level operations using low-level operators to obtain valuable data on Soviet intelligence capabilities have been successfully carried out. One of these has remarkable similarities to Newman's hypothesis that Oswald was used as a dangle to determine gaps in Soviet intelligence.

Indeed, *the same year Oswald defected to the Soviet Union*, the FBI, in conjunction with the Pentagon, recruited another low-level military man to serve as a "dangle" to the Soviets. In this effort (code-named Operation SHOCKER), the U.S. wanted to gather information about the Soviets' nerve gas program and trick them into wasting time and money by taking research paths the U.S. had already investigated and found unusable. In this long-running case (the operation lasted over 20 years), the FBI "lured" the Soviets into recruiting an American soldier as a spy so that the U.S. could artfully use him as a double agent for disinformation and counter-espionage purposes.

Specifically, the FBI wanted to give the Soviets bad information regarding a germ warfare agent the U.S. had abandoned. As James Risen, writing in the *New York Times*, summarized:

> The data concerned a formula that the United States had tried to develop but had then abandoned because it was considered too unstable for weapons use. By giving it to the Soviets, American officials hoped, they would lead Moscow to waste time trying to develop an unusable nerve agent.

Risen continued, summarizing an exposé written about the case:

> The story centers on Joseph Cassidy, an Army sergeant whom the book calls the F.B.I.'s longest-running double agent of the cold war. Selected by the F.B.I. from a pool of noncommissioned officers in 1959 as a "dangle" to lure Soviet intelligence officers to recruit him as a spy, Mr. Cassidy worked as an F.B.I. double agent against the Soviet Union for more than 20 years.

In addition to feeding the Soviets disinformation on chemical weapons, Cassidy's case had other goals:

> His case, code-named Operation SHOCKER, was devised to learn more about Soviet intelligence operations in America and to keep the Russians busy with an American agent under F.B.I. control, rather than with real spies.

Additionally, even more specific goals were

> ...to learn the identities of the GRU's officers in the United States; to discover how it recruited Americans as agents, and how it ran them; and, *by the questions the Russians asked of the source, to learn what gaps existed in the Soviets' knowledge of the American military.* [emphasis added]

As part of this ambitious and sophisticated operation, the agent (code named WALLFLOWER) was provided with carefully chosen classified documents to give the Soviets, to convince them of his authenticity. Wise, author of the exposé about the recently revealed counterfeit traitor case, summarized the sophisticated logistics of the operation as follows:

> Together with the army, the FBI screened and selected a military man to be dangled to the Russians. The bureau ran the agent. The army provided the agent as well as the "feed"—the classified materials to be released. Within the Pentagon, an elaborate system of secret panels reviewed the feed. Ultimately, the Joint Chiefs of Staff approved the documents given to the Russians. The entire procedure was supersensitive and highly secret.

Throughout this 20-plus year operation, the U.S. operative and his Soviet handlers were carefully monitored. According to the book about this American double agent, the clever spy operation was a huge success. As Risen wrote: "the Cassidy case ultimately allowed the F.B.I. to unearth deep-cover Soviet moles operating in the United States who were assigned by the Soviets to work with Mr. Cassidy."[112] The success of the operation was described further by Wise:

> By the questions the Soviets put to WALLFLOWER [Joseph Cassidy], the FBI and the Pentagon discovered a good deal about what the Russians knew and did not know about American military strength and secrets. The United States also learned more about how the Soviets recruited and ran American agents and more about their tradecraft techniques as well, from hollow rocks, new chemicals for secret writing, and rollover cameras, to codes and communications. In addition, the six Soviets sent to handle Joe Cassidy were kept busy running a controlled source, which left them less time to recruit and run real spies.[113]

The double agent in this case was recruited from a pool of U.S. military men in 1959 after being stationed in Japan, *the very same year that Oswald defected to the Soviet Union*[114] *after his service in Japan.*[115] This begs the questions: Was Oswald in the same pool of men and recruited to be a double-agent targeting the Soviet Union? If so, did he also enable the counterintelligence groups in the FBI and CIA to identify Soviet moles they suspected of operating in the U.S.? Additionally, from the questions the Soviets asked him, did they also learn of Soviet gaps in knowledge related to the U-2 spy plane? Could this explain the "special" treatment that Oswald consistently was given and the extensive high-level surveillance he and his files were continually under?

* * *

Following his return to the U.S. from the U.S.S.R. (on a State Department loan), Oswald the alleged Communist sympathizer eventually settled in a right-wing community in Texas composed of ardent anti-Communists where he soon began his highly visible pro-Communist act all over again. This situation in which Oswald exhibited militant *pro-Communist* sentiments while being surrounded by violently *anti-Communist* associates with ties to the CIA would become a familiar one.

Oswald's newly acquired status as a Soviet defector and American traitor, combined with his "pinko" political activities in the U.S., would serve a very useful function for the CIA and its ongoing attempts to smear various left wing organizations within the U.S. as being pro-Communist.[116] In addition to being a useful tool in the CIA's illegal domestic spying operations within the U.S., Oswald would also be a useful tool as part of the CIA's secret war against the Soviet satellite Cuba.

Oswald and the CIA's Illegal Domestic Spying Operations

In his fascinating book entitled *Spy Saga: Lee Harvey Oswald and U.S. Intelligence*, Professor Melanson proposes that Oswald's pro-Communist and leftist behavior upon his return to the United States was not the result of genuine idealism but was instead part of a deliberate plan designed to complement a massive, ongoing domestic spying program on the part of the CIA.

Melanson argues that Oswald was used as part of this ongoing effort[117] both to engage in domestic spying and to justify the need for the CIA's ongoing and illegal domestic counterintelligence program in the U.S.

The justification for this long-running CIA domestic spying operation, which illegally targeted tens of thousands of American citizens, was the assumption that the Soviet Union had infiltrated American politics (especially the 1960s-era peace movement) to a great extent and that therefore the CIA had to spy on American citizens to root out "fifth column" Communists.[118] For example, the CIA counterintelligence agency was determined to find alleged Soviet manipulation of both the anti-war movement during the Vietnam protest years and the black power movement during the civil rights protest era. Through a project code-named CHAOS, which was formally started in 1967, the CIA (in cooperation with the National Security Agency and the FBI) targeted numerous left-leaning dissidents and dissident organizations for illegal infiltration and manipulation.[119] A similar program named MERRIMAC was secretly implemented under the pretext of protecting the CIA from organized domestic unrest allegedly targeting the intelligence agency and its facilities.[120]

Under these two domestic spying programs, thousands of files were opened on American citizens (including four members of Congress), anti-war protesters were followed and photographed, anti-war, peace and civil rights groups were infiltrated, had their offices bugged and mail opened and were otherwise surveilled and spied on.[121] Additionally, as part of these ongoing intelligence-gathering programs, the CIA used its agents and operatives to infiltrate many targeted groups "to learn whatever they could about the organizations, including their domestic sources of funds and the names of those who attended meetings."[122]

In addition to the CIA's domestic spying operations, the FBI had a parallel program named COINTELPRO (shorthand for counterintelligence program). It used its infiltrating agents as *agents provocateurs* to engage in illegal and often violent behavior as a means of discrediting, disrupting and justifying harsh reprisals against the targeted groups. As authors Ward Churchill and Jim Vander Wall summarized:

> This widely used tactic involved the infiltration of targeted organizations with informers and *agents provocateurs*, the latter expressly for the purpose of fomenting or engaging in illegal activities which could then be attributed to key organizational members and/or the organization as a whole. *Agents provocateurs* were also routinely assigned to disrupt the internal functioning of targeted groups and to assist in the spread of disinformation.[123]

By some accounts, the FBI's infiltration of the anti-war movement was even more extensive than the CIA's. After noting that the "use of informants and provocateurs was part of a massive *sub rosa* campaign to subvert the forces of dissent in the late 1960s and early 1970s," Martin Lee and Bruce Shlain gave a summary of the extent of this campaign: "Over a quarter of a million Americans were under 'active surveillance' during this period, and dossiers were kept on the lawful political activities and personal lives of millions more."[124]

The massive effort to manipulate the left was successful. Lee and Shlain describe how government agents were able to incite extreme leftist behavior that was ultimately very useful for cracking down on the peace movement at-large: "Although they did not realize it at the time, the ultramilitants were playing right into the hands of the Nixon administration, which seized upon incidents of violence by protesters to justify the imposition of repressive measures against the antiwar movement as a whole."[125]

* * *

As will be seen, many of Oswald's unusual activities on his return to the United States can be explained as due to participation in a similar, though earlier, CIA/FBI cooperative effort targeting an anti-war effort. Although the CIA was actively participating in covert activities against Vietnam at the time of Oswald's antics,[126] the anti-war effort the CIA was targeting in Oswald's case was that related to the agency's covert war on Cuba.[127]

It is of no small interest that some of the leftist organizations that were later targeted by the CIA's Vietnam-era programs CHAOS and MERRIMAC were the very organizations that Oswald-the-Soviet-defector began lobbying with and for in his pro-Communist actions.

Melanson presents evidence suggesting that Oswald's leftist behavior after his return to the United States was designed to systematically tar these leftist and/or pro-Castro organizations with the appearance of being in league with the Soviets (in Melanson's words, "smearing the left Kremlin-red") to justify subsequent domestic monitoring and infiltration of these groups by the CIA and FBI. This was often accomplished by leaving a paper trail designed to link "independent" left-wing organizations in the U.S. with the Communist Party USA and therefore, through guilt-by-association, with the Soviets. *Oswald himself would form the links between nominally "independent" leftist organizations and Communist organizations through his post-defection political activities.* Oswald's reputation as a militant Communist defector/agitator gave him "leftist credibility" that allowed his personal correspondence to tie numerous American organizations to the Communist Party. And, since Oswald was a famous Soviet sympathizer, his alleged ties to the Communist Party would link them to the Soviet Union.

A revealing pattern emerges from Oswald's leftist activities following his return. Typically, Oswald would join or form an organization that was associated with an organization that the CIA was interested in infiltrating or discrediting due to its alleged Communist control. After attending functions associated with such organizations, Oswald would begin creating a paper trail through letter writing to the U.S. Communist Party. This would conveniently give the appearance that this organization was linked to the Soviet Union via the Communist Party and its dutiful servant Oswald.

Melanson describes one fascinating case in which Oswald suddenly joined the American Civil Liberties Union after attending a meeting with a "friend" while living in Dallas. Ten days later he began writing to the Communist Party USA (which he was not a member of) requesting information on how he might begin to make the ACLU more "progressive."[128] (In one letter to the American Communist Party, Oswald asked: "Could you advise me as to the general view that we have on the American Civil Liberties Union? And to what degree, if any, I should attempt to heighten its progressive tendencies?"[129])

This series of actions created a conspicuous paper trail between a known Soviet defector (Oswald), the Communist Party USA and the independent ACLU. This paper trail, which hinted at an alleged Communist agenda associated with the ACLU (or an ACLU infiltrated by communists), could then be used by the CIA to justify further infiltration and covert manipulation.

Oswald also used his letter-writing act to create a paper trail that is eerily consistent with a designed attempt to discredit an independent political group known as the Fair Play For Cuba Committee (FPCC), a group critical of American foreign policy towards Cuba. For example, while living in New Orleans shortly before the Kennedy assassination, Oswald formed a local chapter of the Fair Play for Cuba Committee after writing to their national headquarters in New York.[130] An indication of a purported discrediting role in Oswald's forming this New Orleans chapter of the FPCC can be found in a letter he wrote to the FPCC shortly after he had drafted some pro-Cuban political circulars for distribution. In this letter to the national director of the FPCC, Oswald wrote that "you may think the circular is too provocative, but I want it too [sic] attract attention, even if its [sic] the attention of the lunatic fringe."[131]

In another correspondence, in this case to the American Communist Party, Oswald requested Communist literature so he could mix it with the literature from the Fair Play for Cuba Committee: "I ask that you give me as much literature as you judge possible, since I think it would be very nice to have your literature among the 'Fair Play' leaflets (like the one enclosed) and pamphlets [sic] in my office."[132] This request for Communist Party literature that could be conveniently mixed with FPCC literature (and his inclusion of FPCC literature with his correspondence) seems tailor-made for linking the FPCC with the Communist Party. Likewise, Oswald's drafting of pro-Cuban circulars with his self-admitted goal of attracting the attention of the lunatic fringe seems perfectly consistent with his being used to discredit the FPCC. (This was convenient, as both the FBI and CIA were keeping close tabs on the FPCC in search of derogatory information.[133])

[It was recently revealed that the treasurer of the Communist Party USA and the editor of the *Daily Worker* were both FBI informants posing as Communists at the time of the Kennedy assassination.[134] These facts, along with the evidence regarding the CIA's and FBI's extensive infiltration of the Communist Party and the Socialist Workers Party, bring up the intriguing question: Was Oswald, while writing to these dissident organizations, actually corresponding with fellow operatives posing as leftists within these institutions?]

Another seemingly innocuous event in Oswald's leftist activities has ties to ongoing domestic CIA operations. This was Oswald's participation in a voter registration effort in Clinton, Louisiana, through a group known as the Congress for Racial Equality (CORE). Oswald may have been serving as an informant in this effort as part of an early version of the MERRIMAC program. The Rockefeller Commission, a presidential commission formed allegedly to investigate Kennedy-era CIA abuses, described techniques used by government operatives to infiltrate and spy on groups within the MERRIMAC program in the following manner:

> They were instructed to mingle with others at demonstrations and meetings open to the public, to listen for information and pick up literature...to attend meetings of the organization, to show interest in their purpose, and to make modest financial contributions.... They were directed to report on how many persons attended the meetings or demonstrations, what they said and what activities were conducted or planned.[135]

According to Melanson, CORE was to become targeted by the MERRIMAC project several years after the Kennedy assassination (as was the Southern Christian Leadership Conference or SCLC[136]). Was Oswald being used to spy on this organization under instructions similar to those revealed by the Rockefeller Commission's investigation as discussed above? Was the presence of the leftist defector Oswald at the voter-registration rally designed to monitor or justify further monitoring of this group along with other black political organizations?[137]

In addition to his actions with respect to the ACLU, FPCC and the CORE, other aspects of Oswald's actions while living in Dallas and Louisiana have a suspicious appearance consistent with an agenda of deliberate provocation. Even the much-debated episode in which Oswald mail-ordered the rifle he allegedly used in the assassination of JFK and the pistol he supposedly used in the post-assassination murder of Dallas police officer Tippit has a link to government operations. Oswald bought the mail-order guns from two companies that were under investigation by a government committee (the Dodd Committee).[138] This committee was seeking to justify gun control due to the ease with which "criminals" were able to obtain them. Since Oswald could have bought guns over-the-counter in Dallas, one wonders whether this mail-ordering activity involving firearms purchases, in addition to leaving a paper trail leading to himself as the future assassin of JFK, was a subset of his general pattern of leaving a paper trail through the mail system as an *agent provocateur* to discredit targets of ongoing government investigations and therefore justify an expanded role for government interference in these organizations. (Recall that the government was monitoring Oswald's mail from the time of his defection to the Soviet Union.)

Oswald and the CIA War Against Cuba

Although these incidents are interesting in light of later CIA programs designed to spy on American organizations and private citizens, it is Oswald's lobbying for pro-Cuban organizations such as the Fair Play for Cuba Committee (FPCC) that provides the strongest evidence he was working within a manufactured leftist pose under the watchful eye of the CIA and FBI.

In 1960, the CIA was frantically preparing an army of Cuban exiles for an invasion of Cuba to remove Fidel Castro from office. When the Cuban invasion failed at the Bay of Pigs in April 1961, the CIA began intensely pursuing other means of removing Castro, such as organizing political resistance within Cuba, creating economic hardship through embargo and sabotage and outright political assassination of Cuba's political leaders. As part of these efforts, the CIA began conducting secret, small-scale military raids against Cuba using the remnants of its Bay of Pigs exile army. The CIA also began recruiting underworld figures for placement in Cuba for assassination attempts as well as recruiting Cuban students in America for placement in Cuba as spies. Much like its late 1960s Vietnam-era activities, the CIA also became intensely involved in spying on and discrediting pro-Cuban organizations within the U.S. as part of its attempts to justify its ongoing efforts to illegally remove the Castro administration from Cuba (much like it had previously overthrown the democratically elected government of Guatemala).[139,140]

It is within this anti-Cuban, post-Bay of Pigs political climate, which included the CIA's *surveillance and infiltration of U.S. groups opposed to this effort,* that Oswald began to engage in pro-Cuban political activities in Louisiana (one of the places the Cuban exile army was illegally trained in the U.S).

As Newman notes, Oswald's pro-Cuban activities during his brief stay in New Orleans (after moving there from Texas just prior to the assassination of JFK) seem to fall into two categories that involved activities under his real name and activities under an assumed name of Aleck Hidell (or A.J. Hidell). The pattern of these activities suggest that Oswald was working under a cover during his stay in New Orleans just prior to the Kennedy assassination and that his pro-Cuba antics were designed firstly as *domestic spying efforts* targeting pro-Castro elements, secondly as *political discrediting efforts* aimed at pro-Castro organizations and thirdly as a means of *setting him up as a fall guy for the murder of John F. Kennedy* (whom many in the CIA unjustifiably blamed[141] for the failed Bay of Pigs invasion and the subsequent failed attempts at removing Castro from office by other means).

The First Phase: Domestic Spying

Many researchers have pointed out the manner in which Oswald's role in his allegedly *pro-Cuban* activities fit in with the CIA's *anti-Castro* agenda (and the FBI's parallel efforts in implementing this agenda). Were Oswald's allegedly pro-Castro activities indeed part of the CIA's anti-Castro operations? If so, what purpose did these activities serve?

FBI and CIA memos from the period indicate much concern over organizations such as the pro-Castro Fair Play for Cuba Committee during the CIA's '50s and '60s-era anti-Castro crusade. CIA memos from the time reveal that as part of its war on Castro's Cuba, the CIA was very interested in monitoring and discrediting the FPCC organization due to its pro-Cuban political stance. However, much like the case of the anti-Vietnam war groups that would be infiltrated within a few years, CIA/FBI investigations were unable to find any evidence of direct Communist control of this independent pro-Cuba organization.

Additionally, the CIA and FBI were concerned that the paramilitary groups and spies it was recruiting and training for anti-Castro activities were in actuality pro-Castro. This was a valid concern.[142] Much effort was undertaken by U.S. intelligence organizations to determine the true loyalties of its operatives in these activities.[143]

It is within this context that Oswald's actions in New Orleans "on behalf of" the FPCC take on a new light.

Newman hypothesizes that Oswald's activities under the assumed name of A.J. Hidell were undertaken as part of a government effort to test the loyalties of Cuban operatives and suspected Castro sympathizers in Louisiana. Newman also proposes that following this period, Oswald's activities under his own name (a known communist sympathizer) were undertaken to discredit the pro-Castro Fair Play For Cuba Committee.

Oswald's pro-Cuban activities during his "Hidell phase" have been suspected by many researchers as being part of a government effort to "smoke out" Communist sympathizers in New Orleans. This was part of an effort to keep the paramilitary and espionage groups it was recruiting free from potential Cuban agents. By forming an organization and posing as a no-name political organizer sympathetic to Castro's Cuba, Oswald could be useful as bait to monitor those individuals who responded to his allegedly pro-Castro political activities or expressed interest in his group.

A major clue as to Oswald's true role in playing the leftist Fair Play For Cuba Committee activist can be found in the New Orleans address printed on some of his Hidell-phase FPCC pro-Castro leaflets. This address, 544 Camp Street, was that of a violently anti-Castro CIA "front" organization staffed by a man named Guy Banister—an ex-FBI agent[144] turned private detective with a long history involving intelligence-related, anti-Castro activities. In New Orleans, Banister was specifically concerned with conducting background checks on recruited anti-Castro operatives[145] to make sure they weren't in actuality pro-Castro agents infiltrating the U.S. anti-Castro operations.[146] Newman proposes that Banister used the "left-leaning" Oswald as a "trap" to lure Cubans in the area with pro-Castro sympathies into exposing themselves.[147] (Unsuspecting Cuban sympathizers responding to Oswald's pamphlets by mail would be unaware they were in fact writing to a militant anti-Communist intelligence office.)

Melanson makes a similar observation: "Banister's modus operandi was in keeping with the style of CIA domestic spying that would later be manifested in CHAOS and MERRIMAC. He hired young men to infiltrate college campuses in New Orleans and search out pro-Castro sympathizers and activists."[148] According to authors Warren Hinckle and William Turner, Banister's widow claimed that extra copies of Oswald's "Hands Off Cuba!" leaflets were found in her husband's office store room.[149] Banister's secretary, Delphine Roberts, claims that Oswald was a frequent visitor to Banister's office and that he had filled out an "agent form."[150]

Upon closer examination, Oswald's utility in the anti-Castro operations of the CIA and FBI cause one to question whether he was indeed being used in exactly the same manner that the CIA used operatives against organizations involved in the Vietnam-era anti-war effort. Might not this alleged targeting of an earlier American anti-war movement using Oswald have been a smaller-scale version of the massive counterintelligence efforts later mounted by the CIA through the CHAOS project to confront and discredit the anti-Vietnam war movement and the "leftist" groups participating in it?[151]

The Second Phase: Political Discrediting

Following this political activity under the Hidell alias, Oswald suddenly began using his real name in his New Orleans activities. He also began a phase of simultaneous pro- and anti-Castro activities that Newman believes were designed to discredit the FPCC in the eyes of the public. For example, after offering his services as an ex-Marine to an *anti-Castro* agent (Carlos Bringuier) working with the CIA to overthrow Castro, Oswald suddenly began handing out his *pro-Castro* leaflets only a few blocks from the operative's store. This resulted in a violent interaction between the two that resulted in the arrest of Oswald and the CIA operative. This arrest served to provide a public spectacle that resulted in much bad publicity for the FPCC.

After the arrest following his highly visible scuffle with the anti-Castro operative, Oswald went on the radio to debate his anti-Castro opponent. During this debate it was dramatically revealed that Oswald was in fact a Soviet defector. This incident linked the supposedly independent FPCC and its pro-Castro leanings with the Soviet Union through Oswald himself.[152] Melanson argues that this incident was manufactured by Oswald[153] to allow Oswald to perform a "discrediting role" in tarring the pro-Castro Fair Play for Cuba Committee as Soviet-controlled.[154]

Oswald's letters to Communist organizations following this incident are intriguing with respect to this hypothesis. After the histrionics surrounding Oswald's public unveiling as a Russian sympathizer and pro-Cuban activist, Oswald once again wrote a revealing letter to the Communist Party USA to tell it that he may have "compromised" the FPCC (he also sent FPCC membership cards to the Communist Party hierarchy). In a letter to the

Central Committee of the Communist Party USA,[155] Oswald made the following statement: "I feel I may have compromised the FPCC, so you see that I need the advice of trusted. [sic] Long time fighters for progress. Please advise."[156] Elsewhere in his correspondence to the American Communist Party, Oswald cogently noted that "Our opponents could use my background of residence in the U.S.S.R. against any case which I join" and that "by association, they could say the organization of which I am a member, is Russian controled, ect [sic]. I am sure you see my point."[157] Indeed.

Newman also proposes that this second phase in Oswald's New Orleans activities prepared him for a sub-phase, which was the reason behind his trip to Mexico City shortly before the Kennedy assassination. It is proposed that this stage was a continuation of the CIA's domestic operations to discredit the FPCC, however, in this case the operation was to take place in foreign countries. Curiously, shortly after the CIA informed the FBI of its desire to discredit the FPCC in foreign countries, Oswald suddenly prepared to travel to Mexico. Newman summarizes this convenient development:

> On September 16, 1963, the CIA "informed" the FBI that the "Agency is giving some consideration to countering the activities of the [FPCC] in foreign countries." In one of the many suspicious coincidences of this case, the next day Oswald was standing in a line to get his Mexican tourist visa. He would take his FPCC literature and news clippings of his FPCC activities with him. In the CIA's memo to the FBI, they said they were interested in "planting deceptive information which might embarrass the [FPCC] Committee in areas where it does have some support." A week later Oswald boarded a bus for Mexico City, where he would represent himself as an officer of the FPCC and use his FPCC card as identification in an attempt to obtain a visa to get to Cuba. This raises the possibility that Oswald's trip was part of a CIA operation or an FBI operation linked to the CIA's request.[158]

This development regarding Oswald's trip to Mexico is interesting in light of CIA director Colby's admission that the activities of some CIA infiltrators and double agents were, in addition to serving espionage purposes, used to prepare them for foreign intelligence missions.[159] Thus, in addition to a discrediting role, Oswald's creation of the local chapter of the FPCC in New Orleans may have served to help establish his left-wing credentials as a means of preparing him for another intelligence mission in a foreign country—in this case Mexico, Cuba or even the USSR.[160]

* * *

This convenient behavior on the part of Oswald leaves many unanswered questions.

Was Oswald a U.S. intelligence mole sent in to spy on the Soviet Union? Were his apparent Communist sympathies the result of hypno-programming along the lines described by Estabrooks? Was his reputation as a Communist sympathizer and defector used to establish his leftist credentials as a means of subsequently spying on suspected pro-Castro leftists in New Orleans and as a cover for acting to discredit these groups in the eyes of the American public? Was Oswald's alleged role as a domestic spy also designed to provide him with leftist credentials to be used in a future discrediting mission in Cuba or the USSR?

The answer to these provocative questions will probably only be found as a result of a new congressional investigation in which complete access to relevant CIA documents is obtained.[161] The available evidence certainly warrants such an investigation.

The Third Phase: Oswald as Hypno-Programmed Assassin

Oswald's activities in New Orleans and Dallas were certainly intriguing. He was constantly surrounded by militant *anti-Communists* (such as those in the White Russian exile groups in Dallas) while engaging in highly visible *pro-Communist* activities. While his activities as a pro-Communist sympathizer may have been related to CIA domestic spying programs, it is also possible that these activities had an even higher purpose: setting him up to take the fall for the upcoming Kennedy assassination.[162] As Melanson observed:

> Oswald's New Orleans summer was indeed productive. It generated negative publicity for the FPCC and was a propaganda coup for the anti-Castroites; it produced a paper trail supporting the Agency's professed theory of communist subversion while simultaneously legitimizing domestic spying. Beyond these payoffs, there was another

one which—whether or not it was specifically intended at the time—would be crucial within three months. Oswald's pro-Castro involvement would be a central element in the purposely crafted image of Oswald-the-assassin.

It is doubtful that Oswald suspected what was about to happen with respect to the imminent murder of President Kennedy and his role in taking the blame for the crime. One might also ask whether Oswald was even aware of the role he may have played in Dallas and New Orleans as part of the CIA's domestic spying efforts and anti-Castro activities. If Oswald's mind had been manipulated to create an anti-Communist "super spy" along the lines described by hypnosis expert George Estabrooks, then Oswald may well have been playing the role of militant pro-Communist unwittingly and unwillingly as a result of having his personality artificially split by the CIA. The same might be said of his alleged role as perpetrator in the Kennedy assassination.

* * *

While there is considerable evidence that Oswald was acting as a double agent or informer after his return the United States, this does not prove that he was doing it under the influence of mind control. However, the striking similarities between Estabrooks' description of a hypno-programmed spy, declassified descriptions of proposed CIA mind-control experiments and the details surrounding the assassination of JFK lend credibility to this thesis.

After testing the feasibility of creating hypnotically controlled assassins, Morse Allen of the CIA eventually asked for permission to conduct "terminal experiments." [163] One under consideration was outlined by John Marks:

> CIA officials would recruit an agent in a friendly foreign country where the Agency could count on the cooperation of the local police force. *CIA case officers would train the agent to pose as a leftist and report on the local communist party.* During training, a skilled hypnotist would hypnotize him under the guise of giving him medical treatment (the favorite ARTICHOKE cover of hypnosis). The hypnotist would then provide the agent with information and tell him

to forget it all when he snapped out of the trance. Once the agent had been properly conditioned and prepared, he would be sent into action as a CIA spy. [emphasis added][164]

This description could fit Oswald as a double agent used to create and/or infiltrate existing left wing organizations in the U.S. under the influence of mind control. Marks' description of such proposed CIA experiments is remarkably similar to the process Estabrooks described for creating an anti-Communist "super spy". It is also chillingly similar to events that occurred while Oswald was behaving in a pro-Communist manner in New Orleans just prior to the Kennedy assassination.[165]

Marks continued in his description of the proposed CIA hypnosis experiment with a programmed double agent:

> Then Agency officials would tip off the local police that the man was a dangerous communist agent, and he would be arrested. Through their liaison arrangement with the police, Agency case officers would be able to watch and even guide the course of the interrogation. In this way, they could answer many of their questions about hypnosis on a live guinea pig who believed his life was in danger.

Now consider the incident that occurred while Oswald was in his pro-Communist pose in New Orleans shortly before the Kennedy assassination. While brandishing a "Viva Fidel" sign and handing out his "Fair Play for Cuba!" pamphlets on a street corner in New Orleans, a scuffle broke out between Oswald and an anti-Castro Cuban whom he had recently offered help in overthrowing Castro.[166] Oswald was immediately arrested, only to be released the next day.[167] Following this incident, Oswald appeared on the radio to explain and defend his Marxist views—an act that helped establish the credibility of his "Marxist traitor" role that would later be useful in pinning the Kennedy assassination on a disgruntled defector and communist sympathizer. The anti-Castro exile Oswald offered his military services to, Carlos Bringuier, was quoted in *Life* magazine as saying: "I was suspicious of him from the start. But frankly I thought he might be an agent from the FBI or CIA trying to find out what we were up to."[168]

In addition to the similarities between Oswald's pre-assassination behavior and the proposed CIA experiment described by Marks, the Kennedy assassination itself bears a resemblance to proposed CIA mind-control/assassination experiments. Consider Marks' description of one such experiment that was to involve a defector turned into an assassin who would be disposed of after the fact:

> According to a CIA document, the subject was to be a 35-year-old, well-educated foreigner who had once worked for a friendly secret service, probably the CIA itself. He had now shifted his loyalty to another government, and the CIA was quite upset with him. *The Agency plan was to hypnotize him and program him into making an assassination attempt. He would then be arrested at the least for attempted murder and "thereby disposed of."*[emphasis added]

Although it is not known whether the proposed terminal experiment involving a defector and an assassination attempt under project ARTICHOKE as described by Marks was ever carried out,[169] think of it in light of the scenario that unfolded in Dallas. Oswald the assassin/defector was disposed of while in police custody after being pinned as the assassin of a prominent American official shortly after his highly visible arrest in New Orleans established him as a disaffected communist radical.[170]

Could Oswald have been used in a similar terminal experiment in Dallas to assassinate, under the influence of mind control, an American official, notably one who had allegedly become a threat to the CIA command structure?[171] The puzzling aspects of Oswald's adult life certainly are consistent with his being a double agent.[172] Such a scenario might explain why an openly "Marxist Marine"[173] was given access to a top secret U.S. naval base in Japan, why a Marine who defected to the Soviet Union[174] and returned to the U.S. was not tried for treason for offering to sell military secrets to the Soviets (in the American embassy, no less), why Oswald subsequently obtained a job at a Dallas-based defense contractor doing highly sensitive photographic work for the army and finally, why he participated in simultaneously pro and anti-Communist political activities while working for one and possibly two[175] ex-FBI agents in New Orleans just prior to the Kennedy assassination.

Was "Oswald-the-leftist" given these jobs because he was not a legitimate threat at all due to the fact that he was actually acting out a role under the influence of mind control in the manner described by Estabrooks? This dual personality theory might also explain why Oswald had multiple ID cards in his possession (his selective service notification and certificate of service in the U.S. Marine Corps)[176] when he was arrested—with the names of both Lee Harvey Oswald and Alek Hidell on them.[177] Could Alek

Hidell (allegedly chosen because it rhymed with Fidel) have been Oswald's alter ego, the pro-Communist "head of the nonexistent chapter"[178] of the Fair Play for Cuba Committee, the personality that infiltrated right-wing gatherings and rallies so that he could report on their activities to the American Communist Party and the ACLU,[179] and the personality that purchased (under the name of Hidell) the mail-order rifle used in the Kennedy assassination?[180]

But these details are not the most compelling evidence of CIA complicity in Oswald's actions as they relate to the death of JFK. There is evidence consistent with the theory that Oswald was in fact a CIA assassin.

Although it was ignored during the Warren Commission's investigation of the Kennedy assassination, evidence has surfaced linking the assassination squads that the CIA was using in its attempts to kill Castro[181] with Oswald and the assassination of President Kennedy. One set of CIA-backed assassination attempts against Castro prior to the Kennedy assassination involved the Mafia, which had lost a tremendous amount of money when their Cuban casinos were shut down by Castro. Oswald was himself connected to the Mafia through his family[182] and had supposedly offered his services to anti-Castro groups planning military exercises against the Castro regime.[183]

In addition to Oswald's ties with *institutions* used in attempts to kill Castro, there are more direct and personal links between Oswald and CIA *assassins*. Recently declassified documents indicate that *Oswald was interacting with one of the very Mafia assassins the CIA had hired to assassinate Castro*. As was recently revealed on the front page of the *New York Times*, the CIA was afraid that the FBI would discover this damning evidence in their surveillance of Oswald:

> The files show how the C.I.A. scrambled hours after the assassination on Nov. 22, 1963, to locate dossiers on Oswald (they found 30). They record a C.I.A. official's fear that the Federal Bureau of Investigation was tailing him *as he met with the mobster the C.I.A. had hired to kill Fidel Castro.*[184] [emphasis added]

Thus, Oswald, who has been presented to the world by the American establishment as a lone nut assassin,[185] was not only being tracked nearly continuously by both the CIA[186] and FBI[187] but also was interacting with CIA-backed paramilitary groups and *even known CIA assassins*. So I ask:

The Perfect Assassin

Was Oswald himself a CIA assassin? And was the assassination of JFK the result of a CIA-orchestrated "terminal" experiment in mind control?[188]

[In addition to association with CIA assassins just prior to the Kennedy murder, Oswald had interactions with a high-level KGB official who worked for the KGB assassination department. Oswald met with this official, Valery Vladimirovitch Kostikov, during his visit to the Russian Embassy in Mexico City, just prior to the Kennedy assassination.[189,190] This official was referred to by a future director of the FBI as "the most dangerous KGB terrorist assigned to this hemisphere."[191] And yet, in spite of all this suspicious activity *under the watchful eyes of the CIA*, Oswald's name did not even appear on a list of dangerous persons in the Dallas area compiled by the Secret Service.]

Anti-Castro Cubans and the CIA: A Hypno-Programmed Mercenary Army?

In addition to the evidence linking Oswald to mind control, the CIA and FBI, there is evidence linking the use of mind-control technology to the anti-Castro paramilitary squads Oswald was interacting with.

CIA researchers involved with these activities admitted contemplating using the MKULTRA technology to kill Castro. As Marks details in his book, a MKULTRA veteran

> admits that he and his colleagues spent hours running the arguments on the Manchurian Candidate back and forth. "Castro was naturally our discussion point," he declares. "Could you get somebody gung-ho enough that they would go in and get him?"[192]

It is of interest that Estabrooks, who gave such a lucid account of how effective it would be to train individual double agents using hypnosis and induced multiple personalities, also gave detailed information of how this technology could be used to train entire mercenary paramilitary groups. Even more to the point, Estabrooks (in his book published before the Bay of Pigs invasion and before the Kennedy assassination) specifically mentioned the brain-washing of disgruntled Cubans for use in covert paramilitary operations:

> Once again let us choose the imaginary aggressive Cubans as examples. In the event of war, but preferably well before the outbreak of war, we would start our organization. We could easily secure, say, one hundred excellent hypnotic

subjects of Cuban stock, living in the United States, who spoke their language fluently, and then work on these subjects.

In a manner similar to that described above, Estabrooks suggested that these exiles could be recruited and manipulated through hypnotism to serve as unwitting spies:

> In hypnotism we would build up their loyalty to our country; but out of hypnotism, in the "waking" or normal state, we would do the opposite, striving to convince them that they had a genuine grievance against this country and encouraging them to engage in fifth column activities. So we build up a case of dual personality.

Thus, not only does the Kennedy assassination bear a likeness to mind-control experiments the CIA was documented to have been carrying out, there is documented evidence that CIA mind-control experts and other hypnosis experts were investigating the use of this technology prior to the assassination on the very group (anti-Castro agents) that Oswald was a part of and that is suspected of playing a significant role in the assassination of JFK.

* * * *

In addition to the Castro assassination operations, there is evidence that the paramilitary force that the CIA raised in operations against Castro has been used as a mercenary army to conduct numerous covert domestic operations inside the U.S.

The 1970s-era *New York Times*' revelations show that the Bay Of Pigs veterans were being used as domestic spies over a long period of time.[193] Operatives involved in the anti-Castro operations and reportedly the Kennedy assassination[194] have been linked by several researchers to scandalous political incidents such as the Nixon-era Watergate break-in[195] and the Reagan-era Iran-Contra scandal. As the authors of *Deadly Secrets* observed:

> It was the war heroes of the Cuba Project who broke into Watergate. Veterans of the Secret War may have played a role in the theft of President Carter's briefing book during

The Perfect Assassin

the 1980 presidential campaign, and they started the back-channel negotiations that led to the Iran-Contra affair.[196]

Thus, in addition to the alleged use of MKULTRA technology to train Oswald for the assassination attempt on Kennedy, this technology may have also been used in the creation and use of this larger force as well.[197] On this topic, questions that come to mind include:

- Was a mind-controlled mercenary group of anti-Castro Cubans set up as described by Estabrooks?
- Were mind-controlled assassins used against Castro as the CIA contemplated doing?
- Was the CIA assassin that Oswald met with under the eyes of the FBI a mind-controlled assassin?
- Was Oswald a subset of this group of mind-control victims?
- If this larger force existed, does it still exist?
- Are there other mind-controlled assassins waiting in the wings?

Jerry Leonard

Part Three

Jerry Leonard

Confirmation of Navy Assassin Training

If Oswald was used as a CIA mind-controlled double agent/assassin, at what point was he "recruited" for such work and how was this recruitment managed? It is of interest that Oswald, being a Marine and therefore under the Navy command structure, would most likely have fallen under Navy auspices for any "spy" programming of the type described by Estabrooks.

Does the Navy have an infrastructure in place for training assassins? In addition to the Estabrooks and Marks revelations of the power that the intelligence community had over manipulating behavior through hypnosis and drugs, a similar revelation of the technology used by the U.S. armed forces to train people to kill without remorse was made in 1975 by the *Sunday Times of London*. The *Times* reported[198] the "confession" of a Navy psychologist named Dr. Narut who was employed at the U.S. naval hospital in Naples. As relayed by *The Times*, Dr. Narut reported that the Navy routinely trained assassins and hit men to kill without guilt or remorse by using techniques designed to desensitize them to violence.[199] Dr. Narut described how pre-selected subjects[200] were recruited among passive-aggressives (including convicted murderers) and forced to watch violent and gruesome films to help them to "heighten their dissociative powers" as well as to teach them to accept violence with emotional detachment. These trained killers were then stationed throughout the world for future service.

Was "Oswald-the-Marine" recruited as part of this Navy program? One possibility is that any psychological tests given to Oswald while he was in the Marines were used to select him for future mind manipulation.[201] Oswald's assignment in Atsugi, Japan, may have been a deliberate placement as part of his "training." This location served as a highly secretive naval base that, in addition to serving as a top-secret U-2 spy plane base, and "one of the CIA's main operational bases in Asia,"[202] also served as a center of mind-control experimentation.[203]

Estabrooks, the hypnosis expert who described in detail how to create a double agent through hypnotically induced multiple personality disorder, not only worked for the military but specifically had ties to the Navy[204] and the Marines. In addition to providing multiple, detailed descriptions of how to program double agents to infiltrate both fascist[205] and Communist groups, Estabrooks even described a successful,[206] real-life use of this technology *to program a Marine* as a double agent to infiltrate communist groups:

> During World War II, I worked this technique with a vulnerable Marine lieutenant I'll call Jones. Under the

watchful eye of Marine intelligence I split his personality into Jones A and Jones B. Jones A, once a "normal" working Marine, became entirely different. He talked communist doctrine and meant it. He was welcomed enthusiastically by communist cells, and was deliberately given a dishonorable discharge by the Corps (which was in on the plot) and became a card-carrying party member.[207]

Manipulating this Marine according to his textbook description, Estabrooks could recover information about the enemy groups his programmed spy had infiltrated: "All I had to do was hypnotize the whole man, get in touch with Jones B, the loyal American, and I had a pipeline straight into the Communist camp."

An even more sophisticated application of hypnosis was to hypnotize a double agent to appear to be hypnotizable by enemy forces when captured. This application would take advantage of the power of hypnosis to create multiple personalities that would be impervious to hostile hypnosis and with the ability to control bodily function so as to be immune to pain and torture as well as control vital signs typically used as indicators of hypnotic trance. This would allow the agent to "record" the hypnosis techniques of the enemy *while appearing to be under their hypnotic control* as well as to give them disinformation while they were convinced that they had "turned" the agent they had captured. Estabrooks described this capability:

> Among the most complicated ploys used was the practice of sending a perfectly normal, wide awake agent into enemy camp, after he'd been carefully coached in waking hypnosis to act the part of a potential hypnotism subject. Trained in autosuggestion, or self-hypnosis, such a subject can pass every test used to spot a hypnotized person. Using it, he can control the rate of his heartbeat, anesthetize himself to a degree against pain of electric shock or other torture.

Estabrooks claims that one of his hypno-programmed agents (another officer in the military) with the pseudonym Cox was used in this way. According to Estabrooks: "Cox worked so well that they fell for the trick. He never allowed himself to be hypnotized during séances." Even better: "While pretending to be a hypnotized subject of the foe, he was gathering and feeding back information."

Oswald's behavior while in Japan fits the pattern of someone being used in a similar manner as a guinea pig in mind-control experimentation. Oswald appeared to live well above his means while living in Japan, routinely cavorting in expensive nightclubs known for catering mainly to officers.[208] Could these clubs have been where his manipulators gave him drugs and monitored his subsequent behavior with female "hostesses" as had been done in American bars and safe houses using CIA-recruited prostitutes during the infamous LSD/MKULTRA testing projects?[209] Estabrooks once again provides a detailed description of the use of this technique in a real situation with his "Officer Cox." In this WWII-era operation, a programmed double agent was "dangled" in front of undercover enemy forces hoping they would take the bait:

> In the case of an officer we'll call Cox, this carefully prepared counter spy was given a title to indicate he had access to top priority information. He was planted in an international café in a border country where it was certain there would be enemy agents. He talked too much, drank a lot, made friends with local girls, and pretended a childish interest in hypnotism. The hope was that he would blunder into a situation in which enemy agents would kidnap and try to hypnotize him, in order to extract information from him.[210]

This description sounds curiously similar to Oswald's activities in Japan where he associated with expensive Japanese prostitutes and escorts[211] in local bars and, to the amazement of his fellow Marines, even had an extremely attractive and apparently Russian girlfriend.[212] Oswald would later confide that he had been associating with Japanese communists in Tokyo during his Marine stint.[213] This begs the question of whether Oswald the Marine was unwittingly following in the steps of Estabrooks' programmed military subject and unwitting "counter spy" Cox.

Other aspects of Oswald's life are consistent with the theory that he was being manipulated even before joining the Marines, perhaps from the time he joined the civil air patrol in New Orleans. The Civil Air Patrol unit Oswald joined prior to joining the Marines provided him with links in the United States to shady characters involved with both the CIA and hypnosis. For example, the head of Oswald's civil air patrol unit, David Ferrie, was reported to have been a pilot supporting covert operations against Castro's Cuba as well as having been involved with hypnosis.[214] In a raid on his apartment following the assassination, authorities reportedly found an extensive library on hypnosis,[215] and eyewitnesses have described hypnosis being used at social gatherings at Ferrie's apartment. (Additionally, Oswald was reported by eyewitnesses to have been a guest at Ferrie's apartment when assassination attempts were being discussed.[216]) This association with Ferrie, the CIA black-ops pilot and would-be hypnotist, may in fact have been Oswald's introduction into mind control and covert activities prior to his joining the Marines.[217] Ferrie may even have been instrumental in getting Oswald to join the Marines. (Ferrie was reported to have encouraged several boys from his Civil Air Patrol unit to join the military.[218])

Oswald's CIA Baby Sitter?

It has been proposed that when the CIA creates a mind-controlled operative it provides a "baby-sitter" or "controller" to coordinate the operative's cover, monitor his activities, provide instructions and watch over him from arm's length to see that he doesn't get into unplanned trouble. Based on his activities in New Orleans, it is reasonable to suspect that his controller there may have been Guy Banister, the former FBI man with naval intelligence contacts.

In addition to Oswald's suspicious activities in New Orleans, there is evidence that he was being manipulated or controlled by the CIA during his stay in Dallas. According to Oswald's wife Marina, Lee's best (and only) friend in Dallas was a man named George De Mohrenschildt, whom *USA Today* described as "a Russian exile with murky ties to the CIA."[219]

The Oswald/De Mohrenschildt friendship was a bizarre one. It is another seemingly contradictory chapter in the Oswald story that seems to make sense only in the light of the theory that Oswald was being handled or "baby-sat" by the CIA. On the surface, the two men seemed about as far apart as two individuals could be. Yet for a brief period they were frequently seen together hob-nobbing with the financial and social elite of Dallas.

The worldly and sophisticated offspring of a Czarist nobleman, De Mohrenschildt was a prominent member of the Dallas White Russian émigré community. He routinely traveled internationally on "business" trips (sometimes for the CIA) and was a co-owner of a corporation named the Cuban-Venezuelan Oil Trust Company that had business interests in Cuba. By comparison, Oswald was born in relative poverty, was considered unsophisticated and uncouth and had a rather obnoxious personality. Yet the globetrotting petroleum geologist with a notorious reputation for being involved in international espionage (including working for a CIA front

The Perfect Assassin

named the International Cooperation Administration) took a spontaneous "liking" to Oswald.

Perhaps there is more to this friendship than meets the eye. De Mohrenschildt's life did have some similarities to Oswald's. For example, De Mohrenshchildt was monitored by both the FBI and CIA throughout his career. In one CIA report he was accused of having both fascist ties and "Communist tendencies."[220] He was also suspected of being a double agent with numerous ties to both friendly and hostile foreign intelligence agencies (including French and German agencies).

Some years after the assassination, De Mohrenschildt committed "suicide" just a few hours after telling an ex-UCLA government professor and author named Edward Jay Epstein that he "had been encouraged to maintain his contacts with Oswald by J. Walter Moore, an employee of the CIA's Domestic Contact Service in Dallas, in 1962."[221] The day De Mohrenschildt committed suicide was also the day he was contacted by an investigator for the House Select Committee on Assassinations—the first *congressional* investigation into the assassination.[222]

Was De Mohrenschildt one of Oswald's baby-sitters? Did he have inside knowledge of the CIA's alleged role in Lee's behavior? This wealthy sophisticate who had at one time been a visitor to the Long Island estate of Jackie Kennedy's parents and who had the name (George "Poppy" Bush) and address of the future Director of Central Intelligence Agency in his telephone register, upon hearing the news of Kennedy's violent death, immediately asked if the suspect's name was Lee Oswald.[223]

Despite continuing revelations, the De Mohrenschildt connection to Oswald and the Kennedy assassination is yet another question mark which will probably only be understood as the result of a genuine and thorough investigation into the CIA's alleged role in Oswald's defection to the USSR, his post-defection political activities and the Kennedy assassination.

A Precedent

If the mind-controlled spy/assassin scenario sounds far-fetched, perhaps a real-life example of how hypnosis was used by an amateur hypnotist to manipulate an unwitting person into similar modes of political, criminal and violent behavior would add some credibility to this hypothesis.

There have been documented cases of anti-social acts being committed under the influence of hypnosis in everyday life. One case is of particular interest because it has numerous parallels to the scenario proposed to explain the Kennedy assassination, including the intentional creation of a multiple personality disorder, post-hypnotic amnesia and post-hypnotic suggestion for participation in both subversive political behavior and socially criminal behavior.

After a thorough review of different theories regarding the feasibility of the use of hypnosis in the creation of anti-social behavior (including several cases where crimes were committed by hypnotists), Paul Reiter in his book *Antisocial or Criminal Acts and Hypnosis: A Case Study* describes one case in which an amateur hypnotist was sentenced to life in prison by a jury in the Copenhagen Central Criminal Court for his role in manipulating his "subject" into committing a bank robbery and a double murder.[224]

The hypnotist in this case was able to artificially split the personality of his subject during hypnosis (while they were both serving time in the same jail cell beginning in 1947 for collaboration with the Nazis) and convince him to take part in subversive activities under the delusion of being a key member of a non-existent, clandestine leftist movement. Eventually, using a bogus political agenda as a pretext, the hypnotist was able to persuade his target to give him huge amounts of his own money (allegedly to fund the activities of the clandestine socialist organization) and, when these funds ran out, to get his victim to commit robbery and murder under the influence of post-hypnotic suggestion. The criminal hypnotist was able to convince his subject that he was committing these unlawful acts under the influence of a guardian spirit named X to further the cause of a self-created, underground political movement called the Danish National Communist Party through which society was to be reformed—eventually resulting in the salvation of mankind.[225]

This documented case was published well *before* the Kennedy assassination in 1963 and would seem to make the notion of Oswald as a victim of a similar plot more plausible.[226] Both cases involve a victim subjected to a form of mind-control in which he is used as a hypnotically manipulated pawn to engage in underground leftist political behavior, and ultimately a double murder.[227,228]

Another Precedent: The Unabomber

There is another case that may represent a precedent for the JFK assassination scenario presented here in its use of unethical psychological manipulation in personality transformation; altering a person's moral system so that one might be induced to commit acts that would have been previously personally abhorrent; inducing an individual to engage in extreme leftist behavior and, desensitizing a person to killing for an allegedly greater good. Like Oswald, this case has ties to a Harvard psychiatrist and the CIA.

It is that of the Unabomber, Ted Kaczynski, a high-profile killer who waged a one-man crusade against technology through a letter-bombing campaign—going uncaught for many years throughout the 1980s and '90s.

In the June 2000 issue of the *Atlantic Monthly*, Alston Chase reveals that the Unabomber was the victim of intensive personality altering procedures during psychological experiments at Harvard University from 1959 to 1962. Chase argues that Kaczynski's radical philosophical leanings and subsequent criminal behavior in assassinations were the result of ruthless personality altering he was subjected to as a student at Harvard (as well as by the curriculum he encountered)[229] by researchers with longstanding and high-level ties to the CIA.

Henry Murray, a former military psychologist[230] turned Harvard professor, subjected Kaczynski to a series of personality disintegrating experiments in the late 1950s based on techniques he helped develop for the Office of Strategic Services (the predecessor to the CIA) during World War II. These traumatic "ego stripping" techniques were developed to measure how a person could be systematically destroyed by stress so that the CIA could use the information to choose agents likely to be resistant to interrogation.[231]

In these experiments conducted on unsuspecting students at Harvard, Murray replicated experiments that he had conducted in the military to measure how recruits reacted to highly stressful situations.[232] Specifically, vulnerable students were deceived into writing out highly personal and intimate details of their young lives—their hopes and dreams, moral beliefs and personal philosophies. They were later told they would be asked to discuss and defend these writings in a laboratory session. When the students naively arrived for the proposed discussion sessions, they found themselves in a room under intense spotlights. As they soon discovered, they had been "set up" for an emotionally traumatizing experience orchestrated by the psychologists in charge of the experiment. As Chase summarized: "The intent was to catch them by surprise, to deceive them, and to brutalize them."

In the lab, the students were strapped into a chair and had electrodes attached to their bodies. The unsuspecting students were then monitored as they were subjected to a confrontational and hostile interrogation session based on the personal information they had been tricked into revealing. As the students' innermost feelings and values were systematically attacked and ridiculed by a sophisticated and aggressive inquisitor, the sessions were recorded on film while instruments recorded the student's bodily responses through electrodes attached to their bodies.

After the initial confrontational event, which Murray himself described as "vehement, sweeping and personally abusive," the students were continuously monitored over the years through psychological tests and follow-up discussion sessions.[233] This was done to measure how their personalities and attitudes were changed by the stressful procedures in combination with the immersion in the curriculum at Harvard, which was geared toward the devaluation of personal moral systems and the ridiculing of the very basis of morality.[234]

According to one study, the specially devised curriculum at Harvard, known as Gen-Ed (for General Education), had a general and measurable effect on the "emotions, attitudes, and even the health of some students." As Chase relates, the curriculum induced predictable changes in the students: They would typically exhibit a "progression from a simplistic, 'dualistic' view of reality to an increasingly relativistic and 'contingent' one." In other words, they would predictably adopt the depraved, morally neutral, value-free system preached through the Harvard Gen-Ed curriculum.

The social scientists who developed the curriculum knew exactly what they were doing. Most likely, this curriculum was consciously designed to be a sophisticated intellectual brainwashing system for the "best and brightest" who would need to be systematically stripped of independent thought and quaint notions of traditional morality before they would go on to serve the power elite in management positions in government and industry.[235] As Chase observed: "By advertising, propaganda, and other techniques of behavior modification, this system sought to transform men into automatons, to serve the machine."

While the curriculum at Harvard did its job on the student body at-large, the "culture of despair" at Harvard, as well as the experiments he was personally subjected to, apparently had a more catastrophic effect on Kaczynksi. As Chase relates, Kaczynski was reported to be well adjusted prior to these Harvard experiments—which Chase described as "disturbing and what would now be seen as ethically indefensible." He had glowing reports from his high school guidance counselor and college advisor. His classmates and friends saw no evidence of feelings of alienation or hostility in him. University psychiatrists also initially gave Kaczynski a clean bill of mental health—the preliminary psychological tests given by Morris showed no sign of abnormal tendencies. However, Kaczynski's condition began to deteriorate after his experience with Harvard's psychology department. He became emotionally troubled through his Harvard years. Kaczynski, himself the victim of mind control, began to see mind-control systems at work at large in society. He became convinced that technology was being used to increasingly enslave man and that therefore he had the obligation to fight the system that was imposed upon himself at Harvard and upon society at-large. Indoctrinated with the "morally neutral" value system of Harvard's curriculum, he became desensitized to the concept of murdering his fellow man for a greater cause.

After graduating from Harvard, Kaczynski went on to get his Ph.D. from the University of Michigan. He then became a professor of mathematics at the University of California at Berkeley before abandoning his academic career to begin a violent underground crusade to save society from the evils of science and technology. After heading out for the wilderness of Montana, in 1978, he began to send out murderous letter bombs of increasing technological sophistication. He was caught in 1995, after his brother recognized his anti-technology writings in the Unabomber's Manifesto.

Chase, who was indoctrinated with Harvard's Gen-Ed curriculum at the same time Kaczynski was (he then went on to get a Ph.D. in philosophy from Princeton and to become a philosophy professor), has an interesting perspective on the Unabomber case. After studying the psychological experiments conducted on impressionable students (including Kaczynski) by Harvard's CIA-affiliated psychologist Murray,[236],[237] Chase argues that Kaczynski, convinced by his Harvard experiences of the nobility and urgency of his cause, was effectively turned into a killer-with-a-cause by Harvard's social scientists. Much like the hypnosis victims described earlier, Kaczynski had his value system warped to the point that he thought not only that extreme measures were necessary to fight his cause but that they were morally justifiable.

After describing the overall workings of how the educational system turns men into killers by creating a crisis mentality and depersonalizing their victims,[238] Chase discussed how the system personally affected Kaczynski: "The Unabomber philosophy bears a striking resemblance to many parts of Harvard's Gen-Ed syllabus. Its anti-technology message and its despairing depiction of the sinister forces that lie beneath the surface of civilization, its emphasis on the alienation of the individual and on the threat that science poses to human values—all these were in the [Gen-Ed] readings." Not only adopting Harvard's social scientists' bleak vision of the future of the world, Kaczynski adopted the morally relative "value system" promoted at Harvard, which allowed him to rationalize the murder of his fellow man. Chase again: "Embracing the value-neutral message of Harvard's positivism—morality was nonrational—made him feel free to murder."

*   *   *

Were CIA techniques used to break down Kaczynski and build him back up with Harvard's depraved, amoral world-view? Whatever the methods used,[239] apparently Kaczynski was emotionally traumatized by Harvard's psychology department, and took the philosophy of Harvard's curriculum to what he considered its logical extreme.

In light of Chase's intriguing research, further study of Kacznyski's case is certainly warranted. Research into the effects of the unethical experiments conducted on his fellow classmates and guinea pigs is also warranted. Alas, the effects of Harvard's curriculum on thousands of leaders who went through its Gen-Ed program in their formative years are also justified. As Chase warned, the effects of the indoctrination system constructed by Harvard's social scientists may have tragic consequences on society at-large: "These kinds of ideas did not affect Kaczynsksi alone—they reached an entire generation, and beyond."

*   *   *

Precedents for CIA-Controlled Leftist Activities

Is it plausible that Oswald was engaged in violent, underground, paramilitary, fake-leftist behavior as a bit-player in CIA/FBI-inspired plots to discredit and preempt independent leftist political movements? A review of several relevant media exposés does suggest that not only has the CIA *sponsored* and *manipulated* leftist behavior of this sort, it has done so successfully, on a grand scale, over long periods of time.[240]

Manufacturing International Leftist Culture
The underground leftwing movement that Oswald both infiltrated and created pales by comparison to other international-scale underground leftist movements that the CIA orchestrated. This secret movement to pre-empt potentially "threatening" leftist behavior in favor of a "Non-Communist Left" was created and maintained through an international network of covert media outlets and global cultural institutions and included some of the leading intellectuals of the post-war period. As explained by Laurence Zuckerman in the *New York Times*, the CIA took this approach because it

> recognized from the beginning that it could not openly sponsor artists and intellectuals in Europe because there

was so much anti-American feeling there. Instead, it decided to woo intellectuals out of the Soviet orbit by secretly promoting a non-Communist left of democratic socialists disillusioned with Moscow.[241]

Those who have difficulty with the theory that the CIA could manipulate a small-timer like Oswald into creating an artificial leftist movement should consider the scale of the CIA's international leftist cultural movement. This movement was created and manipulated by funding the careers of writers and other intellectuals who spoke the words that the CIA wanted a wide audience to hear. According to the *Times*:

> This picture of the C.I.A.'s secret war of ideas has cameo appearances by scores of intellectual celebrities like the critics Dwight Macdonald and Lionel Trilling, the poets Ted Hughes and Derek Walcott and the novelists James Michener and Mary McCarthy, all of whom directly or indirectly benefited from the C.I.A.'s largess.

As part of this monumental psychological warfare effort, the CIA undertook the task of manipulating the existing cultural infrastructure and using it as a vast international propaganda network targeting the intelligentsia as well as the masses. The CIA successfully managed this by *infiltrating* existing cultural institutions where they existed and *creating* new ones that didn't already exist. This allowed the CIA to manipulate and direct existing leftist artistic trends or generate new ones as desired to assist with U.S. foreign policy implementation.

Through a network of secret committees and review boards (such as the Psychological Strategy Board and the Operations Coordinating Board), the CIA manipulated culture from behind-the-scenes[242] to suit its propaganda goals on a grand scale. As part of this endeavor, elite publications were created targeting European intellectuals. Artistic trends were started to blunt Soviet criticisms of inequities in the capitalist way of life. For example, according to the *New York Times*, the CIA "bankrolled some of the earliest exhibitions of Abstract Expressionist painting outside of the United States to counter the Socialist Realism being advanced by Moscow."[243]

Additionally the CIA sought to exploit the arts to counter Soviet accusations of racial inequity in the U.S. According to Frances Saunders: "To this end, psychological warfare experts on the Operations Coordinating Board (in close collaboration with the State Department) established a secret Cultural Presentation Committee whose chief activity was to plan and coordinate tours of black American artists."[244]

To target the masses, the CIA "developed a formal strategy for penetrating the motion picture industry."[245] It infiltrated Hollywood and, working with top-level directors such as John Ford and Cecil B. DeMille, created a covert pressure group to censor negative film stereotypes of the American way of life. This group was also "charged with introducing specific themes into Hollywood films." DeMille reportedly told one high-level CIA agent: "any time I could give him a simple problem for a country or an area, he would find a way of dealing with it in a picture."

According to Saunders, quoting a communication from the Motion Picture Service (MPS) to Cecil B. DeMille (hired as a consultant to the government) the CIA skillfully used the MPS which "employed producer-directors who were given top-security clearance and assigned to films which articulated 'the objectives which the United States is interested in obtaining' and which could best reach 'the pre-determined audience that we as a motion picture medium must condition.' It advised secret bodies like the Operations Coordinating Board on films suitable for international distribution."[246]

There was extensive communication between agents assigned to the Hollywood project and CIA hierarchy regarding the content of movies under consideration. As part of its effort to control movie content, the CIA used its influence to alter at least two Hollywood movie endings with political overtones.[247]

And there was never any danger of running out of money for this monumental effort. To accomplish this goal of creating a non-Communist left under its own control, "the C.I.A. cleverly skimmed hundreds of millions of dollars from the Marshall Plan to finance its activities, funneling the money through fake philanthropies it created or real ones like the Ford Foundation. 'We couldn't spend it all,' Gilbert Greenway, a former CIA agent, recalled. 'There were no limits and nobody had to account for it. It was amazing.'"[248]

Frances Saunders, who wrote an extensive exposé of how the CIA manipulated international leftist culture, documented how the agency orchestrated events through a system of "leftist" front groups, which were funded through a system of both legitimate and CIA-created foundations. Saunders reports that over 170 foundations were used in this massive international effort to infiltrate and manipulate leftist culture. Cultural management on such a grand scale was made easier by the fact that the boards of these foundations were occupied by "the cream of America's social, financial and political establishment" and they overlapped extensively with the publishing and intelligence establishments. As an example, Cass Canfield, a trustee of one of these foundations was reported by Saunders to be "one of the most distinguished of American publishers. He was a director of Grosset and Dunlap, Bantam Books, and director and chairman of the editorial board of Harper Brothers. He enjoyed prolific links to the world of intelligence, both as a former psychological warfare officer, and as a close personal friend of Allen Dulles, whose memoirs *The Craft of Intelligence* he published in 1963."[249]

Thus the CIA had a vast network at its disposal consisting of wealthy corporate titans who in addition to directing publishing and media outlets (see Appendix A) also sat on the boards of powerful cultural[250] and philanthropic institutions.[251, 252] It was not difficult for the men at the apex of this powerful network[253] in concert with the CIA to create and direct an influential institutional base of *fake* leftist cultural and literary organizations and media outlets.

Needless to say, with international literary and cultural clout like this in its history, it is not outlandish to think that Oswald's short-lived leftist letter-writing career was also orchestrated by the CIA for political purposes. And given that the same elite which oversaw CIA operations largely staffed investigations into CIA abuses,[254] it is not hard to see why so little is known about these abuses.

Manipulating International Leftist Politics

In addition to sponsoring non-Communist leftist culture under its own control, the CIA sponsored non-Communist leftist political activities. This allowed the CIA to preempt and control legitimate leftist trends and political parties,[255] as well as to discredit them. Such activities had precedent.

Consider Iran. It was revealed by the *New York Times* in 2000 that the CIA overthrew the government of Iran in 1953 by infiltrating the Communist Party there and subsequently orchestrating a series of actions to destabilize the country through violence and psychological warfare, all the while blaming its actions on Communists.[256]

The U.S. intelligence agencies implemented a plan to destabilize Iran after a nationalist leader (Mohammed Mossadegh) came to power in 1951, shortly after Iran's oil fields were nationalized by its parliament. Claiming that the Mossadegh government was too close to the Communist Party in Iran, and raising fears of potential control of Iran's oil fields by the Soviets, the CIA infiltrated the Communist Party in Iran and began to systematically discredit it through violence and disinformation. For example, according to the *New York Times,* the CIA "directed a campaign of bombings by Iranians posing as members of the Communist Party, and planted articles and editorial cartoons in newspapers."

These activities were part of an effort to overthrow the Mossadegh government in favor of one the CIA was all set to put in power, headed by a CIA puppet now known as the shah of Iran. This was accomplished by the CIA in 1953, after it "stirred up considerable unrest in Iran, giving Iranians a clear choice between instability and supporting the shah."[257]

According to the CIA's own history of its role in the Iran coup in 1953 (exposed by the *New York Times*), its role in the affair was extensive indeed: "agency officers orchestrating the Iran coup worked directly with royalist Iranian military officers, handpicked the prime minister's replacement, sent a stream of envoys to bolster the shah's courage, directed a campaign of bombings by Iranians posing as members of the Communist Party and planted articles and editorial cartoons in newspapers." As a result, the CIA "consolidated the power of the shah, who ruled with an iron hand for 26 years in close contact with the United States."

As related by the *New York Times*, this plan, "code-named TP-Ajax, was the blueprint for a succession of C.I.A. plots to foment coups and destabilize governments during the cold war—including the agency's successful coup in Guatemala in 1954 and the disastrous Cuban intervention know as the Bay of Pigs in 1961."[258]

Recall that it was the CIA's Cuban intervention that Oswald is suspected to have participated in as a fake-communist agitator. Evidence continues to surface indicating the level of effort the CIA had put into justifying actions against Cuba using such fake-leftist discrediting tactics.[259] For example, it was revealed in 1998 that the Department of Defense was considering numerous actions designed to rationalize violence against Cuba in the early 1960s. Covert actions that were under consideration included provoking a war with Cuba by faking a Cuban attack on Latin American countries and bribing Cuban officers into attacking the U.S. naval base at Guantanamo.[260] Such activities were planned to provide a false justification for harsh U.S. military retaliation against Cuba that would include air strikes, a land invasion, the mining of Cuba's coastal waters and the support of agents inside Cuba in fomenting a rebellion against Castro.[261,262]

These CIA activities involving violent paramilitary operations are not relics of the cold war, and they have not stopped. The CIA still uses violent paramilitary organizations and informants throughout the world. Consider Haiti. As the *New York Times* revealed in 1994:

> The leader of one of Haiti's most infamous paramilitary groups was a paid informer of American intelligence for two years and was receiving money from the United States while his associates committed murders and other acts of political repression, Government officials said today.[263]

Keeping with tradition, in addition to maintaining leaders of paramilitary groups *outside* the government on its payroll, the CIA also maintains influential people *within* national governments on its payroll. And it does this successfully on an international scale. In Haiti, in addition to sponsoring leaders in paramilitary groups, the CIA also had more "respectable" government thugs on its payroll. The *New York Times* reported that

> ...leading figures in the Haitian military and police were on the C.I.A. payroll, and Government officials acknowledged...that the Haitian intelligence service, which had been trained by the agency, had turned to drug running and political violence.

In addition to Iran and Haiti, the CIA created and subsidized entire political movements (and their alleged competitors) with unprecedented power throughout Europe, the Caribbean and Asia. The CIA helped create and maintain the massively corrupt, single-party rule of Japan—one of the world's largest economic powerhouses—throughout the post-war period.

Far from an underground movement, the CIA maintained Japan's Liberal Democratic Party as the stabilizing influence in Japanese politics. As Tim Weiner wrote in a *New York Times* article in 1994: "In a major covert operation of the cold war, the Central Intelligence Agency spent millions of dollars to support the conservative party that dominated Japan's politics for a generation." The *Times* reported the views of one U.S. ex-intelligence official involved in the operation who summarized it as follows: "By the early 1960's, the payments to the party and its politicians were 'so established and so routine' that they were a fundamental, if highly secret, part of American foreign policy toward Japan."

Through such manipulation, the CIA was able to create an influential network of politicians under its sway to gather intelligence on Japan and undermine the real Japanese left. By subsidizing the careers of more "conservative" liberal politicians and informants, the CIA was able to maintain a single-party rule in Japan for 38 years—until the party was thrown out due to "a series of corruption cases—many involving secret cash contributions."[264] Thus, by co-opting the real left and using fake leftists under its pay, the CIA prevented legitimate threats to its power in Japan.

Tim Weiner, in his summary of the CIA's manipulation of Japan's political system, wrote: "The C.I.A.'s help for Japanese conservatives resembled other cold war operations, like secret support for Italy's Christian Democrats. But it remained secret—in part, because it succeeded. The Liberal Democrats thwarted their Socialist opponents, maintained their one-party rule, forged close ties with Washington and fought off public opposition to the United States' maintaining military bases throughout Japan." Weiner continued: "The C.I.A. supported the party and established relations with many promising young men in the Japanese Government in the 1950's and 1960's. Some are today among the elder statesmen of Japanese politics."

Not content to co-opt the "liberal" party in power, the CIA—true to form—also infiltrated the more leftist "opposition." According to Weiner, "It infiltrated the Japan Socialist Party, which it suspected was receiving secret financial support from Moscow, and placed agents in youth groups, student groups and labor groups..."[265]

Once again, this is exactly the type of operation that it is proposed Lee Harvey Oswald participated in domestically when he returned to the U.S. from his trip to the Soviet Union.

* * *

The CIA has clearly and successfully manipulated politics and culture on an international basis. Although forbidden by law to do so, the CIA has also manipulated the American political system. One notable case has numerous parallels to the Oswald case and other cases described above involving the infiltration of political movements and anti-war movements. This case involves President Bill Clinton.

As noted previously, there was not always a clear separation between the agents the CIA used in its operations within the U.S. and its operations overseas. In some cases, agents who infiltrated domestic groups in the U.S. used their membership as a means of gaining "leftist credibility" for expanding and continuing their espionage efforts outside the U.S.[266]

In a curious variation on this theme, it appears that American operatives recruited for espionage or infiltration programs in foreign countries were later brought to the U.S. and put to work for the CIA. Harvard Ph.D. Roger

Morris (a former member of the National Security Council), in a best-selling book, revealed that Bill Clinton was recruited by the CIA as an operative[267] while he was attending Oxford. Clinton was allegedly recruited for the CIA's project CHAOS to infiltrate and spy on the anti-war movement[268] abroad during the Vietnam War era. According to several high level CIA officials interviewed by Morris, Clinton was one of many bright young students who, after being recruited overseas as CIA assets, went on to positions of prominence in American politics.

Morris also accuses Clinton of overseeing a CIA narcotics trafficking and money laundering operation in Arkansas during his tenure as governor. This operation was part of an effort to provide weapons to the Contras, a paramilitary counterinsurgency group run by the CIA against the leftist government of Nicaragua. If true, it is possible that Clinton was following in Oswald's "Cointelpro" footsteps by infiltrating anti-war groups, returning to the United States after a mysterious trip to the Soviet Union[269] only to participate in domestic covert actions related to CIA-backed counterinsurgency programs targeting Latin American governments it was attempting to overthrow, and to fundamentally affect U.S. presidential politics.

In Oswald's case, the Latin American nation being targeted by the U.S. counterinsurgency efforts was Cuba.[270] In Clinton's case it was Nicaragua.

Such a scenario may also explain the alleged "compartmentalization" of Bill Clinton's mind.[271] He, like Oswald, coming from a troubled, single-parent home with a domineering mother and unstable father figures, may have been a prime candidate for dissociative programming by the CIA so that he could be used as an asset or double agent in later years.

Jerry Leonard

Part Four

Jerry Leonard

Oswald As Patsy

Many have theorized that Oswald was a "patsy" in the assassination of Kennedy, set up to be in the right place at the right time while a trained professional assassin or assassins committed the actual crime. It is noteworthy that, in addition to using mind-control techniques to create assassins, the CIA was also interested in using these techniques to create unwitting patsies. This potential was discussed within the CIA well before the Kennedy assassination. As Marks reported, a veteran of the CIA MKULTRA program who doubted that a hypno-programmed assassin would be reliable enough to actually carry out an actual assassination

> admits that one of the arguments he uses against a conditioned assassin would apply to a programmed "patsy" whom a hypnotist could walk through a series of seemingly unrelated events—a visit to a store, a conversation with a mailman, picking a fight at a political rally. The subject would remember everything that happened to him and be amnesic only for the fact the hypnotist ordered him to do these things. There would be no gaping inconsistency in his life of the sort that can ruin an attempt by a hypnotist to create a second personality. *The purpose of this exercise is to leave a circumstantial trail that will make the authorities think the patsy committed a particular crime.* The weakness might well be that the amnesia would not hold up under police interrogation, but that would not matter if the police did not believe his preposterous story about being hypnotized or if he were shot resisting arrest. Hypnosis expert Milton Kline says he could create a patsy in three months; an assassin would take him six.[272] [emphasis added]

If Oswald did not do the actual shooting of the president, it is very possible that he could have been manipulated using mind control techniques into setting himself up to take the fall through a series of pre-planned actions to implicate himself in the murder. As veterans of the mind control experiments admitted, creating a patsy was far easier than creating a mind-controlled assassin.

The Walker Incident Explained?

In addition to explaining Oswald's bizarre associations with both pro- and anti-Communists prior to the assassination of Kennedy, mind control and multiple personalities may also explain another oddity in his behavior—his alleged attempted assassination of a militant anti-Communist and former major general named Edwin A. Walker.[273] This event in Oswald's life, juxtaposed with his alleged assassination of a president supposedly at the opposite end of the political spectrum from his first alleged target, has puzzled researchers familiar with the case.

Perhaps the dichotomy in Oswald's behavior can be explained in the same manner as his general behavior was explained—as being due to the intentional creation of violent multiple personalities. If Oswald was truly a victim of operation MKULTRA or a related program and he was induced to shoot the president (accused by some as being soft on Communism) while assuming the anti-Communist personality, he may have been induced to attempt to assassinate General Walker while in his pro-Communist personality as a test or "warm-up" exercise[274] prior to the Kennedy assassination. This exercise could serve as a real-life "terminal" experiment to see if hypnosis could be used to induce two distinct ideologically oriented personalities to commit involuntary assassination attempts against persons with opposite ideological orientations.

Objections to the "Lone Gunman" Theory Refuted

As recently declassified documents indicate, Oswald was far from the lone nut the CIA and FBI have made him out to be. But could he have been the sole assassin?

If Oswald *was* the true and only assassin, what about the stories propagated in the conspiracy-oriented assassination literature of multiple gunmen, Oswald's alleged lack of marksmanship with the "inferior" rifle used in the assassination and Kennedy's gruesome backwards head snap at impact with the final bullet that supposedly proves he was shot from the front? Plausible theories explaining these puzzling aspects of the crime have been proposed by researchers such as Dr. John Lattimer and Dr. Louis Alvarez. The research of these two men should be reviewed by anyone doubting that a lone gunman could have accomplished the shooting feat involved in the Kennedy assassination.

Alvarez, a Nobel prize-winning physicist, has explained in the *American Journal of Physics*[275] how Kennedy's backward head snap is consistent with a "jet recoil" effect that would allow for an object hit by a bullet to move *toward* the direction from which the bullet was fired.[276] Alvarez also conducted an extensive analysis of the Zapruder film (through careful measurement of the camera motion[277]) and concluded that indeed only three shots were fired.[278] Alvarez concluded that approximately eight seconds elapsed during the firing of the three shots. This is about three seconds longer than many conspiracy researchers allot for the shooting and would allow more time for a single assassin to accomplish the three-shot feat.

The work of Dr. Alvarez dovetails with the ballistics tests conducted by Lattimer,[279] a physician who did extensive ballistics analysis with the same model rifle[280] used by Oswald to show that three shots could have been fired by Oswald[281] with the required accuracy[282] in the required time.

Lattimer also provides an elegant argument for how the so-called "magic" bullet that pierced Kennedy's throat could have injured both Kennedy and Connally in the manner described by the Warren Commission.[283] His analysis is based on the *actual* alignment of the two victims (Connally and Kennedy) as the shot was fired (versus the straight ahead alignment typically shown by critics of the Warren Commission) as well as an extensive set of experiments demonstrating how a single bullet could have slowed and tumbled after passing through the two bodies (simulated by Lattimer using pig necks) thus producing the multiple injuries in the two men without significant deformation of the bullet.[284]

With the arguments that are typically (and erroneously) used to discredit the lone gunman scenario out of the way, it should be seen that it is entirely feasible that Oswald alone accomplished the shooting in the assassination of Kennedy. However, based on the evidence presented in earlier sections, it should also be readily seen that even if such an act was *physically* committed by Oswald, the CIA could very well have provided the hidden *mental* stimulus for his anti-social response.

Such a scenario involving a CIA hypno-programmed "throw away" assassin would provide definite advantages for the CIA. Through a mere temporary dropping-of-the-guard by the Secret Service, a lone assassin could be "filtered in" to commit political murder for the CIA and take the fall. The crime of eliminating a political enemy of the CIA could be pinned on a single "fall guy" with a history of apparent mental instability (reinforced by the pre-programmed, pre-assassination behavior) or with an apparent grudge against the murdered victim while the CIA stayed out of the picture far above the fray. There would be no multiple gunmen required; no post-assassination alterations of the victim's body to hide the role of multiple gunmen required; no chance of a camera catching an extra gunman in the act; and no slew of eyewitnesses to be murdered after-the-fact. All that would be required would be a single pre-marginalized assassin, ready to commit the act and take the scripted fall.[285]

Summary

"Only a people who refuse to permit themselves to sink into intellectual lethargy and conformity, only a people who question and think...can be sure that hypnosis—disguised or direct—will not undermine their freedom and rob them of their very lives." [286]
 -George Estabrooks

It is documented that the CIA was involved in training anti-Castro Cubans for military operations against Castro[287] and that they had attempted several times to assassinate Castro.[288] Many powerful persons associated with these anti-Castro operations within the CIA power structure had a reason to hold a grudge against President Kennedy. In addition to Kennedy's perceived obstructionism regarding the Cuban operation, Kennedy had forced the dismissal of CIA-director Allen Dulles,[289] as well as his deputy director Charles Cabell over the failed CIA-backed invasion of Cuba at the Bay of Pigs. JFK also created hard feelings within the agency when he began micro-managing CIA covert operations through his brother Bobby Kennedy, the Attorney General.

In addition to the CIA, several other powerful groups were both extremely anti-Castro as well as anti-Kennedy. These groups included disgruntled Mafia families whose gambling operations had not only been destroyed when Castro took control of Cuba (this is why the CIA recruited the mafia in its anti-Castro crusades) but whose gambling operations were being aggressively investigated in the U.S. by Robert Kennedy.[290]

If the CIA was setting up hit squads and training them in the U.S. to get Castro, why couldn't they have used these same squads to eliminate a U.S. president whom they viewed as standing in their way of assassinating Castro?[291] And, given the relevance of this anti-Castro operation to the Kennedy assassination,[292] why was this question not asked by the Warren Commission?[293] These questions take on added significance when you realize that the alleged assassin of JFK had long-standing ties to groups and individuals who were not only involved in the CIA's anti-Castro crusade but were training in the United States in the same timeframe.

As part of its covert operations "bag of tricks," the CIA had spent many years trying to develop the capability of creating involuntary assassins through mind control.

It has been shown that there are many aspects of the CIA's mind control program that have parallels in the assassination of a president of the United States. For example, experiments were planned involving the use of defectors as unwitting assassins who could be conveniently eliminated while in police custody following their assassination attempts. Options were discussed for such experiments that involved using agents in "friendly" countries as well as using them against American officials.

Hypnosis experts published descriptions of the creation of unwitting operatives and double agents using hypnotic suggestion well before the Kennedy assassination. The personality traits of such double agents appear to fit those of Oswald and could explain much of his mysterious dual loyalties and bizarre behavior.[294] Military hypnosis expert Estabrooks had even described using such technology with U.S. Marines, Cuban exiles and paramilitary groups. The CIA apparently considered using this technology to assassinate Castro. (In addition to engaging in behavior patterns consistent with being a CIA operative, Oswald was known to have interacted with these groups that were specifically mentioned as being candidates for mind control and CIA assassins.)

Were mind-control techniques used by the CIA in live "experiments" involving the use of programmed "defectors" to kill a common enemy (Kennedy) in a "friendly country" (the U.S.) because he would not fully cooperate with a program to kill another common enemy (Castro)? Was the CIA assassination/coup operation targeting Cuba redirected to Kennedy and America?[295]

This hypothesis has numerous advantages over conventional theories. It could explain many of the curious details in our current knowledge of the assassination[296] while simultaneously eliminating heretofore-puzzling differences in the various hypotheses presented by the Warren Commission and "conspiracy" researchers. This theory also provides fertile ground for further conspiracy-oriented research while simultaneously eliminating the need to completely discard the research of the Warren Commission and other studies that claim that the assassination could have been performed by a single assassin from the Texas School Book Depository.

In summary, it is hoped that the theory proposed in this study will not only provide a new way of looking at established facts regarding the assassination of John F. Kennedy but will inspire new avenues of investigation. As ever-greater numbers of government documents are declassified, this theory may provide a framework for making sense of confusing and seemingly contradictory aspects of the investigation. Perhaps it will even play a part in pointing out the need for a truly independent congressional investigation into the assassination—one that includes an investigation into the CIA's program for training involuntary assassins.[297] And conceivably such an investigation will determine that Lee Harvey Oswald was indeed the personification of the CIA's successful use of psychological warfare and violence to overthrow democratically elected governments throughout the world,[298] in this case the government of the United States.

Jerry Leonard

Conclusion

"We need to understand the CIA and its allies." [299]
—L. Fletcher Prouty

The *New York Times* recently reported on the slaying of an American citizen in Guatemala by a Guatemalan military officer who was on the CIA's payroll:

> The acting Director of Central Intelligence said today that the C.I.A. should have told Congress three years ago that it had information implicating a Guatemalan colonel on its payroll in the killing of an American citizen, but that the facts had "slipped under the carpet." [300]

The killer is a product of a U.S.-backed training school for Latin Americans called the School of the Americas which, according to the *Times*, is referred to by "its most severe critics" as "an academy of assassins." [301]

Although it is no doubt wishful thinking to hope that the CIA would ever "come clean" if it were indeed similarly involved in training the assassin of an American president, perhaps one day in the not-too-distant future (assuming assassination investigators force the issue) this same establishment newspaper[302] will run a similar story replacing the words "Guatemalan colonel" with "American ex-Marine corporal" and "American citizen" with "American president." The story might appear as follows:

> The acting Director of Central Intelligence said today that the C.I.A. should have told Congress over thirty years ago that it had information implicating an ex-Marine corporal on its payroll in the killing of an American president who had just fired both the director and deputy director of the CIA, but that the facts had "slipped under the carpet."

The parallels between the Kennedy assassination and proposed CIA experiments from the 1950s involving assassination by mind-controlled agents and the convergence between CIA-backed hit squads and President Kennedy's enemies do indeed raise compelling questions that need to be addressed.[303] President Johnson himself, although for different reasons, said this shortly before his death on the subject of the assassination: "I never believed that Oswald acted alone, although I can accept that he pulled the trigger…We had been operating a damned Murder Inc. in the Caribbean."[304]

APPENDIX A

The CIA and the Press: Complicity in the JFK Assassination Cover-Up?

Over the years following the Kennedy assassination, many people have expressed incredulity at the notion that a CIA-inspired covert action that resulted in the death of an American president would not have been uncovered and reported on by the U.S. press. Such a belief overlooks the extent to which the mass media has been infiltrated and manipulated by the intelligence community throughout the Cold War period.[305] This belief is also based on a superficial understanding of both the lack of desire and the lack of legal freedom the media has to report on intelligence-related matters. Indeed, there are numerous precedents for stories far less damaging to the CIA than its role in the Kennedy assassination being quietly and systematically suppressed.

Sarah Lyall, writing in December 1998 in the *New York Times*, reported that, "In Britain, journalists say, the intelligence services have traditionally enjoyed cozy relations with a select group of editors and reporters, who provide sympathetic coverage in exchange for special access and exclusive stories."[306] This statement was prompted by allegations that the editor of the British paper the *Sunday Telegraph* was a British spy for MI6. Although Lyall seems to think it is, this close relationship between the intelligence infrastructure and the media is not restricted to Britain. The extensive and decades-long CIA influence over the U.S. media has been used to great effect for numerous purposes over the last several decades including: censoring news stories about CIA power and covert operations throughout the world, spreading CIA propaganda both internationally and domestically and gathering intelligence through journalists stationed throughout the world.

In the 1970s, several mainstream press outlets including the *New York Times*, the *Columbia Journalism Review* and *Rolling Stone Magazine* published extensive investigations of CIA-manipulation of the media that revealed an amazing degree of intelligence control over reporting and reporters.[307] Over a period of three days in 1977, the *New York Times* published seven articles on the breadth of CIA-infiltration of the mass media as part of its far-flung intelligence gathering and propaganda operations.

The first article, published on Christmas day, revealed the following information regarding the CIA's influence over newspapers, publishing houses and journalists:

- "The C.I.A. has at various times owned or subsidized more than 50 newspapers, news services, radio stations, periodicals and other communications entities, sometimes in this country but mostly overseas, that were used as vehicles for its extensive propaganda efforts, as 'cover' for its operatives or both. Another dozen foreign-based news organizations, while not financed by the C.I.A., were infiltrated by paid C.I.A. agents."

- "Nearly a dozen American publishing houses, including some of the most prominent names in the industry, have printed at least a score of the more than 250 English-language books financed or produced by the C.I.A. since the early 1950's, in many cases without being aware of the agency's involvement."

- "Since the closing days of World War II, more than 30 and perhaps as many as 100 American journalists employed by a score of American news organizations have worked as salaried intelligence operatives while performing their reportorial duties."[308]

As the *Times* disclosed, this level of CIA infiltration of the media and the corresponding influence over information was not limited to the United States. The CIA had created an international media empire/propaganda machine that included the use of many news outlets, reporters and editors all over the world. As John Crewdson of the *New York Times* summarized:

> "We 'had' at least one newspaper in every foreign capital at any given time," one C.I.A. man said, and those that the agency did not own outright or subsidize heavily it infiltrated with paid agents or staff officers who could have stories printed that were useful to the agency and not print those it found detrimental.[309]

In fact, the CIA's influence in the international media was probably much greater than its influence in the U.S. This was because the CIA was prohibited by law from certain actions in the U.S.,[310] whereas it was relatively unrestrained outside the country.

Investigations into the relationship between the media and the CIA have consistently exposed a pattern of high-level cooperation between the two institutions through both *formal* and *informal* channels. Formal channels of cooperation existed through outright CIA-ownership and control of media outlets, news wires and publishing outlets as well as through having paid CIA agents pose as journalists at legitimate media outlets.

In addition to the many news organizations that the CIA owned outright, there were many others, including those in the elite establishment media such as the *New York Times*[311] and *Washington Post*, with which the CIA had much *informal* influence. This informal influence[312] was useful at one level for *gathering* information through the routine debriefing of reporters on their return from overseas assignments[313] and through having open access to the photo libraries and archives of numerous press organizations.

At higher levels, informal cooperation between the CIA and corporate media executives was often instrumental in *censoring* the publication of information that the CIA found objectionable. This informal cooperation was made easier by the fact that, in addition to the cozy relationship shared between the CIA and reporters,[314] the executives at many of the nation's largest press outlets such as CBS, the *New York Times*, the *Washington Post, U.S. News and World Report, Time, Newsweek* and *Life* magazines were intimate friends with individuals at the highest levels of management at the CIA. The *New York Times* summarized in 1977 that "most C.I.A. directors, especially Richard Helms and the late Allen Dulles, have been close friends with the chief executives of some of the nation's most influential news organizations."[315] Kathryn Olmsted, who did her Ph.D. thesis on the subject of the relationship between the intelligence community and the press, was more specific with respect to the ties between the CIA elite and the elite that owned and managed establishment papers such as the *Washington Post* and the *New York Times*:

> For example, Post editor Ben Bradlee's brother-in-law was [CIA] covert operations chief Cord Meyer; Post publisher Phil Graham was probably the closest friend of Frank Wisner, the man who directed the Agency's propaganda machine; and the Times publishing family, the Sulzbergers,

socialized with CIA chiefs Allen Dulles, John McCone, and Richard Helms."[316]

The media-elite and the government-elite shared a similar worldview that, in addition to long-standing social ties, also made informal cooperation much easier, especially when it came to national security-related issues. As media-scholar Olmsted observed:

> From the 1940s to the 1960s, journalists and politicians alike had shared common assumptions about the Communist threat and the need to protect the operations of America's clandestine soldiers in the Cold War. At times, news organizations had censored themselves to keep these secrets. Many publishers and editors socialized with the Ivy League-educated CIA officials and believed strongly in the integrity of these men. They accepted CIA Director Richard Helms's 1971 statement, made in a speech to newspaper editors, that "the nation must, to a degree, take it on faith that we…are honorable men devoted to her service."[317]

The common worldview, background and interests of the media and CIA-elite made deep-felt suspicion of the CIA's motives and operations on the part of the press rather rare. Few in the media would dare to publicly accuse their establishment counterparts in the intelligence world of CIA-backed assassinations of foreign leaders, let alone the assassination of an American president. As Olmsted noted: "For journalists who had gone to the same schools and the same parties as the top CIA brass, it was hard to believe that these men could be threatening the Republic."[318]

* * *

Media cooperation with the CIA (and the intelligence community as a whole) was also made easier by the "revolving door" between the CIA and the media corporations that allowed reporters and media managers to rotate between jobs as CIA employees or operatives and "objective" journalists.[319]

The *Columbia Journalism Review* related that, at the time its exposé was published, the Pentagon correspondent for *US News & World Report*, the *Newsweek* diplomatic correspondent in Washington, the publisher of the *New Republic* and the executive editor of the *Philadelphia Bulletin* (a former Newsweek staffer) were all ex-CIA employees. (Robert J. Myers, publisher of the *New Republic,* had been a CIA station chief in Southeast

Asia.) In addition to these ties documented by the *Columbia Journalism Review*, it has become well known that William F. Buckley, long associated with the founding of the "conservative" *National Review*, had been a former CIA agent.[320] Tom Braden, a syndicated columnist and later "liberal" co-host of CNN's Crossfire program,[321] had not only been hired early on as future director Allen Dulles's assistant at the CIA[322] but had headed up the original CIA program designed to use the media for propaganda purposes[323] (note the CIA's bipartisan media influence[324]).[325]

Authors Hinckle and Turner note that *Life* magazine's publisher, C.D. Jackson, had been "president of the CIA's Free Europe Committee in the 1950s and was also special assistant to President Eisenhower for psychological warfare working on anti-Communist propaganda for Eastern Europe."[326] Frances Stonor Saunders referred to Jackson as "one of the most influential covert strategists in America." Having been "one of America's leading psychological warfare specialists" during World War II, his new position as a top-level advisor to Eisenhower made him "an unofficial minister for propaganda with almost unlimited powers."[327]

Eisenhower's choice to head up the U.S. psychological warfare effort was Nelson Rockefeller, who had extensive and extremely high-level ties to both the intelligence establishment and the media. For example, Rockefeller had chaired the powerful National Security Council committee, which was responsible for overseeing the CIA's covert activities. He later served as the head of a presidential committee investigating abuses of the intelligence agencies. This position conveniently allowed Nelson to control what facts the public was allowed to see with respect to CIA abuses (including political assassinations) that occurred *while he was overseeing the agency*.[328] Rockefeller's position on the presidential investigative committee presented a major conflict of interest since the CIA abuses investigated by Rockefeller's commission included the mind-control studies that were conducted on the American public by the CIA. These mind-control studies were conducted while Rockefeller chaired the CIA oversight committee that was briefed on plans for the human experimentation, many of which were conducted through the department of Health Education and Welfare (HEW) and often funded through Rockefeller foundations at the time Rockefeller was heading up HEW.[329]

In addition to his impressive connections to the intelligence world, Rockefeller's connections with the media were substantial. The Rockefeller family dynasty had influence over numerous powerful media corporations through its long-running control of Chase Manhattan Bank (where David Rockefeller, Nelson's brother, was director). During the controversy over Nelson Rockefeller's appointment as vice president by President Gerald

Ford, the *Washington Post* noted the rather large potential for undue Rockefeller media influence through Chase:

> If the television networks give "Vice President" Rockefeller a bad time, he might turn to a friend at Chase Manhattan. According to a Senate subcommittee's study of corporate ownership, the bank controls respectable minority blocks of stock in CBS, ABC and NBC, not to mention modest bites of The New York Times and Time-Life, Inc.[330]

In addition to the flow of personnel from the intelligence world to the media, traffic also went the other way. For example, Wallace Deuel, Washington correspondent for the Chicago *Daily News* and St. Louis *Post-Dispatch*, joined the CIA in 1953. Joseph Goodwin, a former Associated Press Washington correspondent, joined the CIA in 1966 and Richard Helms, a former United Press correspondent, became director of the CIA during the Johnson administration.

In an interesting three-step process, Joseph Ream left his job as an executive vice president at CBS to take a job as the deputy director of the super-secret National Security Agency, which many researchers believe to be far more powerful than the CIA. As deputy director, he was responsible for the day-to-day operations of the NSA. After his stint at this extremely powerful position (which he listed as "retirement" in his CBS bio), he returned to head up CBS's Washington office. He later headed up CBS's programming department.[331]

* * *

In 1974, the *Columbia Journalism Review* noted hypocrisy inherent in the "non-reporting" by journalists on the subject of CIA-influence in the media:

> American journalists relentlessly pursued every allegation they could find in the 1960's to document the Central Intelligence Agency's infiltration of student organizations, trade unions and foundations. Yet, when it was reported last November that newsmen themselves were on the payroll of the CIA the story caused a brief stir, and then was dropped.[332]

The *CJR* continued: "The journalistic failure to investigate the CIA's use of the news business contrasts sharply with the aggressive exposure of ethical tangles in non-journalistic institutions."

The clubby atmosphere that existed at the apex of the American establishment no doubt made it difficult for one component of the establishment (the press) to seriously question another part (the intelligence establishment). As Olmsted summarized:

> In short, the news media in the 1950s and 1960s had close ties with the CIA as an institution and with the Ivy League alumni who ran it. They went to the same colleges, attended the same dinner parties, joined the same country clubs, and shared the same assumptions about the CIA's role in the world.[333]

Olmsted went on to observe: "As Tom Wicker has pointed out, the press, as a member of the establishment, does not want to risk establishment disapproval."[334]

The journalistic failure to investigate the CIA's use of the news business described by the *Columbia Journalism Review* does in fact have major ramifications for a democracy. As it was later put by the *New York Times*:

> ...using reporters as agents offends and confounds the principles of American democracy. Under constitutional protections, the press is the chronicler of and check on government, not its instrument. If the United States Government does not honor that distinction, who anywhere will believe it really exists?[335]

Indeed.

The extensive CIA media infiltration and manipulation does make one wonder as to whether there is a worthwhile distinction between the press and the government. It also gives pause as to whether the cozy relationship between the press and the CIA threatens the free flow of information necessary for the functioning of a healthy democracy.

Blurring the distinction between the government, the CIA and the press certainly makes it easier for the CIA to suppress uncomfortable facts and threatening stories. At critical times during the Cold War, the CIA was able to use its influence with the media to do just that by censoring articles which threatened to shed light on its day-to-day operations and its role in instigating international events (such as the overthrowing of democratically elected governments) through covert activities. In some cases, CIA management put pressure on publishers to suppress stories. In many cases the media simply censored itself. In other cases, the press outlets themselves voluntarily submitted CIA-related stories to the CIA for editing prior to publication.

An example of this latter form of self-censorship occurred when the editors of *Collier's* submitted an impending article about the operations of a network of overseas CIA "front" companies to the CIA management for censorship prior to publication. In a similar manner, the *New York Times* submitted an exposé of the CIA it was preparing (ironically, on the subject of whether the CIA constituted an invisible government) to the ex-director of the CIA, who deleted parts of the story.

Another example of media publishers censoring their own work occurred when the publisher of the *New York Times,* Arthur Hays Sulzberger, helped the CIA out in a time of need by reassigning a *Times* reporter whom the CIA feared might expose its impending overthrow of the democratically elected government of Guatemala. In another case, the CIA managed to prevent the publication of an exposé in the *Miami Herald* on its preparations for the Bay Of Pigs invasion. Two of these events, the overthrow of the regime in Guatemala and the Bay of Pigs invasion, bear indirectly on the Kennedy assassination.[336] But there are more direct ways in which the CIA has attempted to suppress the dissemination of information relevant to its alleged role in the JFK assassination. One of these methods included direct media-orchestrated propaganda campaigns to discredit vocal critics[337] who dared suggest that the CIA might have had a hand in the killing of Kennedy.

The three-day *New York Times* exposé published in 1977 provided a glimpse into a CIA-run disinformation campaign aimed at rogue "conspiracy theorists." According to the *Times*, one campaign was conducted after the CIA unsuccessfully tried to persuade the publishers of Random House to let it buy up an entire run of an unflattering book about the agency entitled *The Invisible Government*. The CIA reportedly used its influence with editors and reporters in the media at-large to initiate a propaganda campaign[338] "to encourage reviewers to denigrate the book as misinformed and dangerous."[339]

This was not the only time that the CIA initiated a smear campaign to denigrate authors of books critical of the CIA. In fact, *it initiated such a campaign specifically targeting authors who adopted a conspiratorial viewpoint of the Kennedy assassination.*

On December 26, 1977, the *New York Times* published an article about the numerous ways in which the CIA attempted to discredit Kennedy assassination conspiracy theorists. Powerful people in the agency were upset over the fact that various independent researchers were suggesting Oswald might have been working for the CIA and that the Warren Commission had done a less than honorable job in its report by insisting that Oswald was a "lone-nut assassin."[340] To confront and discredit these theories,[341] a memo was dispatched from CIA headquarters to encourage its agents and operatives to use their influence with the press to refute and discredit such arguments.[342] Consequently, a large propaganda operation was implemented to attack critics of the Warren Commission as amateurish, self-interested[343] and in some cases even Communist-inspired.[344]

In addition to supplying ready-made, CIA-friendly arguments about the Kennedy assassination, the agency recommended attacking conspiracy theorists through book reviews and press articles as part of its disinformation campaign.[345] CIA headquarters recommended that agents use influence with editors and politicians to discourage the international dissemination of such conspiracy-minded assassination theories.[346]

The CIA was not the only federal agency relevant to the Kennedy assassination that actively attempted to manipulate and control the press. The FBI also routinely engaged in covert media manipulation to influence public opinion. This included cultivating cozy relationships with "friendly" reporters and editors, planting stories in the press that were favorable to the FBI and campaigning to get stories killed that were critical of the agency.[347] Techniques also included targeting individuals and groups for discrediting or disruption through the media.[348]

One technique for discrediting was opening FBI files on targeted individuals to journalists so that derogatory stories could be printed. In one case that created a stir within elite journalistic circles, the FBI offered the surveillance tapes it had made of Martin Luther King to several reporters in the hopes that they would spread derogatory information about the civil rights activist.[349]

Like the CIA, the FBI targeted critics of its investigations for discrediting and censorship.[350] And like the CIA, the FBI attempted to use the media to discredit critics of the establishment line on the Kennedy assassination. For example, the Senate Select Committee on Intelligence Activities reported that the FBI tried to discredit a public meeting about the Kennedy assassination by maligning a member of the audience:

After a public meeting in New York City, where "the handling of the [J.F.K. Assassination] investigation was criticized," the F.B.I. prepared a news item for placement "with a cooperative news media source" to discredit the meeting on the grounds that "a reliable [F.B.I.] source" had reported a "convicted perjurer and identified espionage agent as present in the audience."[351]

* * *

The intricate web of press outlets and personalities that the CIA owned or influenced has been effective at suppressing news of the various illegal activities that the CIA has engaged in over the years.[352] It is not difficult to see that such a level of control would come in handy to prevent disclosure of illegal acts committed in the U.S., such as complicity in the assassination of a president.

Olmsted, writing in *Journalism History,* relates how members of the media censored themselves when given a sensitive briefing by President Ford about CIA assassination plots against foreign leaders,[353] as well as how considerable pressure was brought to bear on a *New York Times* Pulitzer Prize-winning reporter named Seymour Hersh who broke the story of the CIA's illegal domestic espionage and surveillance efforts within the United States (through the CHAOS project described earlier).[354] Even greater abuse was piled on then-CBS reporter Daniel Schorr, who leaked news of a classified congressional report critical of the CIA.

These efforts on the part of the CIA and their willing accomplices in the media to suppress stories relating to its misdeeds and mistakes[355] hold valuable lessons for students of the Kennedy assassination.

If, as is suggested, Oswald was involved in illegal, U.S.-based CIA spying activities against Cuba and pro-Cuban American groups that, in some shape or form were still ongoing in the 1980s,[356] then similar national security considerations would come into play in any attempts on the part of the press to expose Oswald's role in these operations.

If reporters such as Seymour Hersh, who had leaked news of the CIA's ongoing infiltration of undercover agents into American dissident groups, and Schorr, who had illegally leaked classified House Select Committee on Intelligence reports and news of the CIA's assassination efforts against foreign leaders, were scorned and punished by their self-righteous peers and bosses in the establishment media, one can only imagine what might happen to a "lesser" journalist who leaked secret information that a famous CIA-backed operative was not only involved in the infiltration of American political groups *but* was also the assassin of an American president. (This of course assumes that such a journalist's editor and publisher would print such a blockbuster story to begin with…thereby risking the wrath of their colleagues in the intelligence establishment.)[357]

In addition to these considerations, there is another dimension, a legal one, to the problem of the media's lack of freedom to freely report information about Oswald's alleged connections to the CIA with respect to the Kennedy assassination. If Oswald was indeed an operative with ties to sensitive or ongoing CIA covert operations, or even if he was an independent traitor who had revealed sensitive information to the Soviets, it may actually have been illegal for the press to report on his connections to the CIA or the extent of the CIA's knowledge and monitoring of his "illegal" actions. Such reporting could have compromised ongoing operations, spying capabilities or sensitive networks of informants and operatives.

Such considerations restrained media coverage of the Pelton spy trial in the 1980s. In fact, William Casey, the director of the CIA, threatened to prosecute the *Washington Post* "if it published an advance story on the Pelton trial, which went into details about the eavesdropping operations he allegedly revealed to the Soviets." Similar restrictions and considerations[358] might very well have applied to the Oswald case if he had been involved in a sensitive CIA-sponsored mission into the Soviet Union involving the U-2 reconnaissance plane (for example, if he had revealed sensitive information to the Soviets about the plane) or if he had been a part of a CIA anti-Castro network within the United States. (This latter consideration is especially relevant since such networks were reportedly operational well into the 1980s.) Similarly, it may be illegal to report on the sensitive methods used to track and monitor Oswald during his stay in the Soviet Union.

* * *

Although the extensive CIA use of the media was supposed to have ended in 1977 when an executive order was signed that restricted such abuses, more recent reports indicate this law restricting CIA-infiltration of the media had loopholes that allowed the CIA to continue to covertly infiltrate the media. *USA Today* related in 1996 that "the CIA has secretly waived the law, which also covers members of the clergy."[359] (No mention was made of how the CIA obtained the power to secretly waive U.S. laws designed to regulate its actions.)

According to Stansfield Turner, ex-director of the CIA, journalists have on rare occasions been used by the CIA despite the alleged ban (which, according to Gerald Seib, writing in *The Wall Street Journal* "generally discouraged the practice but allowed for exceptions.")[360]

As troubling as these violations of the spirit of the law have been, even more disturbing developments are in the works. Barriers between the CIA and the press, as permeable they are, may soon be torn down completely. A study group of the prestigious Council on Foreign Relations recommended in early 1996 that the law restricting CIA infiltration of the press be rescinded and that the CIA be given free reign to infiltrate the media once again.[361] This decision has been justifiably criticized by journalists writing in the *New York Times*[362] and the *Wall Street Journal*,[363] mostly because they themselves had been incorrectly accused of being spies while on assignment in Iraq and Iran respectively and recognized the inherent danger of such CIA/media manipulation to other U.S. journalists (who might also be falsely accused and unjustly punished) working abroad.

The decision by the influential Council on Foreign Relations has unfortunately emboldened the CIA to reconsider actions that have long-been controversial, including covert use of the media. *USA Today* reported during the height of the recent debate on CIA use of the media before a congressional committee that "CIA director John Deutch said …he'll recruit journalists as spies when he feels it's necessary."[364]

Given what is at stake, it is a sad state of affairs that the establishment press outlets such as the *New York Times* have not reported more extensively on these proposed changes in legislation that would seriously corrupt journalism at the hands of the intelligence agencies.[365] Alan Saracevic, writing in *Mother Jones*, provided a fitting summary of the current situation (as well as the historic one) when he noted: "The *Times*, it appears, is afraid of being too hard on our intelligence agencies. That includes the FBI."[366]

Conclusion

Given such widespread CIA and FBI media influence,[367] it is no wonder that the shortcomings of the Warren Commission's conclusions and the deliberate CIA misrepresentation of the facts before congressional investigative committees have gone unreported for so long by the establishment press. In light of the information summarized above, it should be obvious that any serious investigation into the assassination of President Kennedy would be incomplete without an uncensored investigation into CIA and FBI manipulation of the press. A good place to start would be to declassify the material the Church Committee buried on the subject.

Jerry Leonard

About the Author

Jerry Leonard is a physicist who has been actively involved in microelectronics research and production for over fifteen years. He has numerous patents and publications related to his scientific career. Mr. Leonard has been studying the documented history of Nazi Germany, the eugenics movement and unethical government experimentation related to viral cancer research and mind control research on human subjects for over ten years.

END NOTES

[1] Irving L. Janis, "Are the Cominform Countries Using Hypnotic Techniques to Elicit Confessions In Public Trials?," U.S. Air Force, Project Rand Research Memorandum, RM-161, 25 April, 1949, p. 20.

[2] As will be seen in this study, there is considerable evidence supporting the theory that the Kennedy assassination was carried out as part of the Mafia/CIA assassination operation against Castro. Many of the same personalities in these organizations with the means and motive to kill Castro appear to have been involved in the Kennedy assassination. As authors Warren Hinckle and William Turner note: "The major figures in the John F. Kennedy assassination were, in one way or another, connected to the Cuba Project–to the CIA, or the mob, or, as was more often the case, to both." Warren Hinckle and William Turner, *Deadly Secrets: The CIA-MAFIA War Against Castro and the Assassination of J.F.K.*, (New York: Thunder's Mouth Press, 1992), p. 16.

[3] See for example the Warren Commission Report or Gerald Posner's *Case Closed*– a recent defense of the Warren Commission report that trivialized theories proposing that Oswald had substantive ties to organized crime or the intelligence establishment. Posner's book was greeted with great fanfare and cheering by the establishment press (much like the Warren Report), and much disgust and derision by the "conspiracy establishment." [For comparison see Gerald Posner, *Case Closed* (New York: Anchor Books, 1993) and Harold Weisberg, *Case Open: The Omissions, Distortions and Falsifications of Case Closed* (New York: Carroll & Graf Publishers, Inc., 1994)]

[4] N. Horrock, "CIA Documents Tell of 1954 Project to Create Involuntary Assassins," *New York Times*, 2/9/78

[5] To support this theory, evidence will be presented based on public information that existed prior to the assassination as well as formerly classified material (which has been made public over the years since the assassination) concerning the CIA's assassination and mind-control programs.

[6] Quoted in Bowart, *Operation Mind Control*, Freedom of Thought Foundation, Limited Researcher's Edition, (#131), 1995, PO Box 35072, Tucson, AZ 85740-5072, Back Cover.

[7] Edward J. Epstein, *Legend: The Secret World of Lee Harvey Oswald*, (New York: McGraw-Hill Book Company, 1978), p. 137.

[8] Oswald's avowed political stances could be strikingly contradictory. As Gerald Posner reports: "Émigrés remember that if he was talking to someone who was a right-winger, he advocated Communism, and in front of leftists, he praised fascism." Posner, p. 86.

[9] This is the scenario that horrified the Warren Commission to the point that it considered keeping the record of its deliberations from the public, lest it lose faith in these institutions. As it turned out, this is now a moot point.

¹⁰ This scenario was dramatized in *The Manchurian Candidate,* a novel written by Richard Condon and published in 1959 about an American soldier who was turned into an unwitting assassin of a political candidate through communist mind-control techniques after his patrol was captured by the Chinese in the Korean War. A Hollywood movie by the same title was later released based on the book. Interestingly, in an interview at the end of the home rental version (available from Blockbuster Video circa 1994) of the 1962 movie *The Manchurian Candidate,* Frank Sinatra (who starred in the movie) and the producer-writer George Axelrod discussed the fact that President Kennedy was intensely interested in the details of the movie project.

¹¹ N. Horrock, "CIA Documents Tell of 1954 Project to Create Involuntary Assassins," *New York Times,* 2/9/78

¹² L. Fletcher Prouty, a high-level ex-government insider intimately involved with the planning and execution of international covert operations (as Chief of Special Operations Office for the Joint Chiefs of Staff in charge of coordinating military activities to support CIA covert operations) hypothesizes that JFK was executed for his reluctance to escalate the Vietnam war as desired by the American military/industrial "super power elite." (This was a major theme of Oliver Stone's conspiracy-intensive film *JFK.*) Perhaps the JFK assassination was a "trigger mechanism" for a "bigger project" which turned out to be stepped-up U.S. intervention in Indochina. See chapter entitled "Why Vietnam" in his 1992 book L. Fletcher Prouty, *JFK. The CIA, Vietnam and the Plot to Assassinate John F. Kennedy* (New York: Carol Publishing Group, 1992.

¹³ T. Weiner, "Papers on Kennedy Assassination Are Unsealed, and '63 Is Revisited," *New York Times,* 8/24/93

¹⁴ In a recently published book based on volumes of newly declassified documents, an assistant professor at the University of Maryland named John Newman details the extensive and continuous surveillance (by agencies such as the CIA, FBI, Naval Intelligence & Marine Intelligence) that Oswald was under from the time of his defection to the Soviet Union up to the Kennedy assassination. As will be discussed in a later section, Newman proposes that Oswald was being used as a tool in sensitive CIA counterintelligence operations involving the Soviet and the Cuban governments. See: John Newman, *Oswald And The CIA* (New York: Carroll & Graf Publishers, Inc., 1995).

¹⁵ N. Horrock, "Private Institutions Used in C.I.A. Effort to Control Behavior," *New York Times,* 8/2/77

¹⁶ "Project MKULTRA, The CIA's Program of Research In Behavioral Modification," *Joint Hearing Before the Select Committee on Intelligence and the Subcommittee on Health and Scientific Research of the Committee on Human Resources,* Ninety-Fifth Congress, First Session, August 3, 1977, p. 390.

¹⁷ Ibid., p. 391.

¹⁸ Walter Bowart, *Operation Mind Control* (New York: Dell Publishing Co., Inc. 1978); John Marks, *The Search for the "Manchurian Candidate"* (New York: W.W. Norton & Company, 1979); Gordon Thomas, *Journey Into Madness, The*

True Story of Secret CIA Mind Control and Medical Abuse (New York: Bantam Books, 1989); Martin Lee and Bruce Shlain, *Acid Dreams: The Complete Social History of LSD: The CIA, The Sixties, and Beyond* (New York: Grove Weidenfeld, 1985).

[19] S. Budiansky, E. Goode, T. Gest, "The Cold War Experiments," *U.S. News & World Report*, January 24, 1994, p. 34; V. Fisher, "Altered States of America," *Spin*, vol. 9, no. 12, March 1994, pp. 50-88.

[20] Projects THIRD CHANCE and DERBY HAT were international versions of MKULTRA in which the CIA conducted extensive testing in Europe and the Far East. "Project MKULTRA, The CIA's Program of Research In Behavioral Modification," p. 411.

[21] Olson "was a high-ranking division administrator holding the titles assistant division chief and director of plans and assessments" at Fort Detrick, the center of the government's biowarfare research program. "Prior to that, according to military and CIA records, he served as the division's director of planning and intelligence activities and as director of the SO division itself for about 12 months." H.P. Albarelli Jr. and John Kelly, "New evidence in Army scientist's death 48-year-old case has links to CIA's secret experimentation program," *Worldnetdaily.com*, 7/6/01.

[22] This researcher, Frank Olson, died in 1953 after plummeting from the 10th floor of the Manhattan hotel he was staying in. Olson had allegedly gone to New York to seek therapy for depression that was induced (unknowingly to him) as a result of CIA mind-control doctors surreptitiously giving him 70 micrograms of LSD at a meeting. While the deadly fall was initially labeled a suicide, this convenient verdict has come under intense scrutiny. Olson was traveling with CIA personnel who were keeping a close eye on him after his negative reaction to the CIA-administered drugs (a CIA official was found sitting in Olson's room when the police arrived at the death scene). Additionally, researchers who exhumed Olson's body have claimed that the injuries to Olson's skull were more consistent with a blow to the head *prior* to the "fall" than with injuries from the fall itself. Researchers have also found reason for suspicion that Olson was chosen for the mind-control experimentation because he had become a security risk as a result of moral objections to the research he was engaged in, which involved among other things, "a prototype project involving simulated exercises aimed at biological-contamination of the New York City water supply." H.P. Albarelli Jr. and John Kelly, "New evidence in Army scientist's death 48-year-old case has links to CIA's secret experimentation program," Worldnetdaily.com, 7/6/01; Ted Gup, "The Coldest Warrior," *Washington Post*, 12/16/01; H.P. Albarelli Jr. and John Kelly, "Evidence builds in CIA-related death 'Suicide' of scientist preceded secret deal between federal agencies," *Worldnetdaily.com*, 7/19/01.

[23] "New evidence emerging from the five-year grand jury investigation into the 1953 death of CIA biochemist Frank Olson reveals concerns about several additional puzzling deaths." H.P. Albarelli Jr. and John Kelly, "Mid-century deaths all linked

to CIA?, New evidence in Olson case suggests similarities with other incidents," *Worldnetdaily.com*, 9/4/01.

[24] The CIA official (Sidney Gottlieb) who oversaw the entire CIA mind-control program that resulted in numerous deaths was present the night Olson was given the LSD. He was later "awarded the Distinguished Intelligence Medal, one of the CIA's highest honors." Ted Gup, "The Coldest Warrior," *Washington Post*, 12/16/01

[25] CIA personnel later told the Olson family that high-level researchers like Olson were experimented on "to understand what would happen if 'the enemy' should dose captured American scientists." Olson may have been specifically targeted because "the agency enjoyed a liaison relationship with the scientists at Fort Detrick that made them particularly convenient subjects." It has subsequently been determined that the CIA also had a special deal with the Justice Department which would limit investigation into CIA-related deaths. Thus, the CIA had special relationships with government agencies that allowed them not only to experiment on their employees but also to cover up the results of these unethical experiments. H.P. Albarelli Jr. and John Kelly, "New evidence in Army scientist's death 48-year-old case has links to CIA's secret experimentation program," *Worldnetdaily.com*, 7/6/01; Ted Gup, "The Coldest Warrior," *Washington Post*, 12/16/01; H.P. Albarelli Jr. and John Kelly, "Evidence builds in CIA-related death 'Suicide' of scientist preceded secret deal between federal agencies," *Worldnetdaily.com*, 7/19/01

[26] The experiments conducted in this research were often conducted in civilian hospitals on unwitting patients under the pretext of evaluating the treatment of schizophrenia and other mental disorders. Much of the research was published in the open medical science literature.

[27] As it was described in a Rand Report on the Soviet uses and misuses of hypnosis: "Hypnosis was used as a device for producing emotional disturbances in order to observe their behavioral consequences." Irving L. Janis, "Are the Cominform Countries Using Hypnotic Techniques to Elicit Confessions In Public Trials?" U.S. Air Force, Project Rand Research Memorandum, RM-161, 25 April, 1949.

[28] As Irving Janis wrote in a Rand Report on the subject of whether the Soviets were using this technique to elicit false confessions in their so-called show trials, "a hypnotized subject will often accept and confess to an implanted memory as a real event in his own past life." Irving L. Janis, "Are the Cominform Countries Using Hypnotic Techniques to Elicit Confessions In Public Trials?" U.S. Air Force, Project Rand Research Memorandum, RM-161, 25 April, 1949, p. 5.

[29] R. Brickner, R. Porter, W. Homer, J. Hicks, "Direct Reorientation of Behavior Patterns in Deep Narcosis (Narcoplexis)," *Archives of Neurology and Psychiatry*, vol. 64, number 2, August 1950, pp. 165-195.

[30] C. Farnsworth, "Canada to Pay the Victims of Mind-Altering Treatment," *New York Times*, 11/19/92

[31] Ibid.

[32] Ibid.

[33] Colin Ross, *BLUEBIRD: Deliberate Creation of Multiple Personality by Psychiatrists*, (Richardson, TX: Manitou Communications, Inc. 2000), p. 183.

[34] John Marks, *The Search for the Manchurian Candidate* (New York: W.W. Norton & Company, 1979), p. 67.
[35] Ross, p. 78, 79.
[36] Ross summarized: "Medical experimentation by the Department of Psychiatry at McGill resulted in death, psychosis, vegetable states, organic brain damage and permanent loss of memory among other damages. It resulted in the creation of amnesia, identity disturbance and depersonalization among other dissociative symptoms. Dr. Ewen Cameron was the main figure in these activities." Ross, p. 136.
[37] C. Farnsworth, "Canada to Pay the Victims of Mind-Altering Treatment," *New York Times*, 11/19/92.
[38] Thomas, *Journey Into Madness*, p. 132.
[39] Ross, p. 129.
[40] Ross, p. 81.
[41] Ross, p. 156.
[42] A. Weitzenhoffer, "The Influence of Hypnosis on the Learning Processes," *Journal of Clinical and Experimental Hypnosis*, vol. 2 1954, pp. 191-200.
[43] A. Silverstein, G. Klee, "The Effect of Lysergic Acid Diethylamide on Digit Span," *Journal of Clinical and Experimental Psychopathology*, vol. xxi, no. 1, March. 1960, pp. 11-14.
[44] C. Franks, D. Trouton, S. Laverty, "The Inhibition of a Conditioned Response Following Arecoline Administration in Man," *Journal of Clinical and Experimental Psychopathology*, vol. xix, no. 3, Sept. 1958, pp. 226-233; S. Fisher, "An Investigation of Alleged Conditioning Phenomena Under Hypnosis," *Journal of Clinical and Experimental Hypnosis*, vol. 3, 1955, pp. 71-103.
[45] I. Rothman, "Clinical Use of Drugs in Induction and Termination of the Hypnotic State," *Journal of Clinical and Experimental Hypnosis*, Vol. V, No. 1, January 1957, pp. 25-31.
[46] Having the ability to use hypnosis to overcome the effects of drugs might allow the CIA to train its intelligence agents to thwart the efforts of enemy intelligence agencies to trick them into talking through the use of alleged "truth drugs" such as LSD.
[47] S. Fogel, A. Hoffer, "The Use of Hypnosis to Interrupt and to Reproduce an LSD-25 Experience," *Journal of Clinical and Experimental Psychopathology*, vol. xxiii, no. 1, March, 1962, pp. 11-16.
[48] Other than hypnosis applications, there were numerous reasons why the CIA was interested in the use of drugs. For example, the CIA could use the surreptitious administration of drugs to induce erratic behavior in political figures or the general public as a way of discrediting them. Similarly, the CIA could use the surreptitious administration of drugs to make a person more vulnerable by destroying his marriage or alienating him from his family. Additionally, drugs could be used to create a dependency state that would give the CIA control over the individual.
[49] Although these experiments involving such phenomena as the "reorientation of behavior patterns" and "depatterning" were allegedly conducted to cure mental

illness, numerous investigative writers have suggested how easy it was to use this technology for more sinister ends by the CIA and other military intelligence agencies interested in controlling and manipulating human behavior. A former staff assistant to the Director of Intelligence and Research of the CIA named John Marks wrote a powerful book about the true aims of this secret, long-running mind control program based on declassified documents he was able to obtain through the Freedom of Information Act. This book, entitled *The Search for the Manchurian Candidate,* described the various mind control programs that the CIA initiated and continued throughout the 1950s, '60s and '70s including Projects MKULTRA and ARTICHOKE. For those readers interested in learning more about the research conducted under these projects, Marks' book provides an excellent overview.

[50] Ted Gup, "The Coldest Warrior," *Washington Post,* 12/16/01.

[51] Ross, p. 84.

[52] The hypocrisy is multiplied by the fact that the U.S. began funding mind-control research that was a continuation of the research that the Nazis conducted. Ewen Cameron's research was part of this effort. Cameron may have been one of the doctors given the task of not only investigating but continuing the progress made by the Nazis. Ross related: "In 1945 he was part of an American team that did psychiatric assessments of German war criminals including Rudolph Hess, who was examined at the request of the Military Tribunal in Nuremberg. Dr. Cameron must have heard about the mescaline research done in the death camps by Nazi psychiatrists. He himself instituted similar work at McGill when he began experimenting with LSD." Ross, p. 129.

[53] Couriers are people who transfer secret information from one location to another.

[54] For a general overview of the phenomenon by a CIA psychiatrist see for example: M. Orne, "On the Mechanisms of Posthypnotic Amnesia," *The International Journal of Clinical and Experimental Hypnosis,* 1966, Vol. XIV, No. 2, pp. 121-134.

[55] Posthypnotic amnesia has been a well-known phenomenon associated with the hypnotic trance since 1784. See E. Hilgard, L. Cooper, "Spontaneous and Suggested Posthypnotic Amnesia," *International Journal of Clinical and Experimental Hypnosis,* vol. XIII, No. 4, 1965, pp. 261-273; L. Huesmann, C. Gruder, G. Dorst, "A Process Model of Posthypnotic Amnesia," *Cognitive Psychology,* vol. 19, 1987, pp. 33-62.

[56] Experts in the field claim that subjects can be hypnotized in a manner that not only allows them to carry volumes of information unwittingly, but to resist hypnosis by enemy forces.

[57] George Estabrooks, writing on the security risks typically associated with human couriers and the advantages that a hypnotic courier would provide observed: "But if he is given the message while he is in hypnotic trance, and commits it to memory at that time, the situation is very much altered. Because he does not know, consciously, that he has the message, he cannot be tortured or cajoled or bribed into giving it up. He has nothing to tell, nothing to sell, nothing to say." George H. Estabrooks and

Nancy E. Gross, *The Future of the Human Mind*, (London: Museum Press Limited, 1961), p. 224.
[58] Ibid.
[59] Quote from Estabrooks in *Science Digest* reprinted in: Colin Ross, *BLUEBIRD: Deliberate Creation of Multiple Personality by Psychiatrists*, (Richardson, TX: Manitou Communications, Inc. 2000), pp. 167-170.
[60] Colin Ross, *BLUEBIRD: Deliberate Creation of Multiple Personality by Psychiatrists*, (Richardson, TX: Manitou Communications, Inc. 2000), p. 163.
[61] For reviews of this controversial claim see: A. Sears, "A Comparison of Hypnotic and Waking Recall," *Journal of Clinical and Experimental Hypnosis*, vol. II, 1954, pp. 296-304; M. Erdelyi, "Hypnotic Hypermnesia: The Empty Set of Hypermnesia," *The International Journal of Clinical and Experimental Hypnosis*, Vol. XII, No. 4, October 1994, pp. 379-389.
[62] Ross, p. 38.
[63] Described by the *Post* as "one of the most effective—if unheralded—spies of World War II," Jeannie, who was later decorated by the CIA, used her formidable memory to relate information gained during interactions with German officers (as a translator for the French industrial syndicate) to produce "precise reports on the German's secret military plans, particularly the development of the V1 flying bombs and V2 rockets, [which] helped persuade Prime Minister Winston Churchill to bomb the test site at Peeneemunde and blunted the impact of a terror weapon the Nazis had hoped would change the course of the war." David Ignatius, "After Five Decades, A Spy Tells her Tale," *Washington Post*, 12/28/99.
[64] Seymour Fisher, "The Use of Hypnosis in Intelligence and Related Military Situations," Study SR 177-D, Contract AF 18 (600) 1797, Technical Report No. 4, December 1958, Bureau of Social Science Research, Inc. 2017 Connecticut Avenue, N.W. Washington, D.C.
[65] Ibid., p. 8.
[66] One well-documented aspect of a deep hypnotic trance is a subject's ability to withstand intense pain such as burns with an open flame or puncture wounds with needles. This aspect of hypnosis has routinely been used to perform dental extraction and painful surgery under hypnosis without anesthetic. See: R. Dorcus, "The Use of Hypnosis as a Substitute for Pharmacological Agents," *Journal of Clinical* and *Experimental Hypnosis*, vol. V, no. 1, Jan. 1957, pp. 12-24; F. Marcuse, G. Phipps, "A Demonstration of Dental Extraction With Hypnotic Anesthesia," *Journal of Clinical and Experimental Hypnosis*, vol. IV, Jan. 1956, pp. 2-4.
[67] Fisher, p. 18.
[68] R. Kampman, "Hypnotically Induced Multiple Personality: An Experimental Study," *The International Journal of Clinical and Experimental Hypnosis*, Vol. XXIV, No. 3, pp. 215-227.
[69] Ross reported that such experiments may have been related to CIA/FBI programs to recruit operatives at an early age by the CIA.
[70] Fisher, p. 18.

[71] Estabrooks boasted in an article published in an April 1971 in *Science Digest*: "One of the most fascinating but dangerous applications of hypnosis is its use in military intelligence. This is a field with which I am familiar through formulating guide lines for the techniques used by the United States in two world wars." Quote from Estabrooks in: Colin Ross, *BLUEBIRD: Deliberate Creation of Multiple Personality by Psychiatrists*, (Richardson, TX: Manitou Communications, Inc. 2000), p. 167.
[72] G. H. Estabrooks, *Hypnotism* (New York: E. P. Dutton, 1957), p. 201.
[73] Despite the labor involved in such a process Estabrooks noted that the rewards would be well worth the trouble: "The proper training of a person for this role would be long and tedious, but once he was trained, you would have a super spy compared to which any creation in a mystery story is just plain weak."
[74] By placing government agents or operatives within a given group or movement to act in a violent or socially unacceptable manner, the whole group or movement can be smeared or discredited in the eyes of the public. Such agents are frequently referred to as *agents provocateurs*.
[75] Umberto Eco, *Foucault's Pendulum*, (New York: Ballantine Books, 1990), p. 392.
[76] For an example of the use of "agents provocateurs" to discredit movements such as the civil rights movement, see: "The CIA, the FBI and the Media," *Columbia Journalism Review*, July/August, 1976, pp. 37-42.
[77] Neil Lewis, "FBI Data Show Castro Wary on Kennedy Death," *New York Times*, 3/31/95
[78] Interestingly, one of these agents posing as an American Communist Party leader obtained detailed information from a meeting with Fidel Castro relating to Castro's own investigation of the JFK assassination. As a result of this investigation, Castro supposedly concluded that Oswald could not have acted alone in the assassination.
[79] A. H. Lubasch, "316 Used By F.B.I. In Informer Role," *New York Times*, 9/5/76
[80] George H. Estabrooks and Nancy E. Gross, *The Future of the Human Mind*, (London: Museum Press Limited, 1961), p. 223.
[81] Ross, p. 163.
[82] George H. Estabrooks and Nancy E. Gross, *The Future of the Human Mind*, (London: Museum Press Limited, 1961), p. 211.
[83] In a recent article describing the massive mind control experimentation conducted by the CIA, the *Washington Post* described the man who headed up the program—Sidney Gottlieb—as "the CIA's sorcerer," who had "attempted to raise assassination to an art form." Ted Gup, "The Coldest Warrior," *Washington Post*, 12/16/01
[84] See: M. Erickson, "An Experimental Investigation of the Possible Anti-Social Uses of Hypnosis," *Psychiatry*, vol. 2, 1939, pp. 391-414.
[85] It should be noted that hypnotists have vested financial and professional interests in maintaining the public's trust in their profession. This may explain why the party line on this subject is so slavishly adhered to by the hypnosis community. After all, how many people would place themselves under the control of a hypnotist if it were

widely assumed that such a person had the power to induce them to engage in objectionable behavior?

[86] M. Brenman, "Experiments in the Hypnotic Production of Anti-Social Self-Injurious Behavior," *Psychiatry*, vol. 5, February, 1942, pp. 49-61.

[87] See section: "Cases From Criminological Literature of Crimes Committed Under Hypnosis" in Paul J. Reiter, *Antisocial or Criminal Acts and Hypnosis: A Case Study*, (Copenhagen: Munksgaard, 1958), pp. 53-66.

[88] M. Kline, "The Dynamics of Hypnotically Induced Anti-Social Behavior," *Journal of Psychology*, vol. 45, 1958, pp. 239-245.

[89] George H. Estabrooks and Nancy E. Gross, The Future of the Human Mind, (London: Museum Press Limited, 1961), p. 218.

[90] Ironically, one of the psychiatrists that programmed double agents for antisocial behavior used this same rationalization for his own antisocial behavior. Convincing himself that "War is the end of all law," and that, "in the last analysis any device is justifiable which enables us to protect ourselves from defeat," George Estabrooks confessed to engaging in such antisocial behavior by developing various hypnosis applications for military purposes: "For developing some of them, the senior author of this book, to whom the military applications of hypnosis have always been of interest, must plead guilty, and if the effort to discover means of helping one's country in time of war is antisocial, then he has engaged in antisocial behavior." George H. Estabrooks and Nancy E. Gross, The Future of the Human Mind, (London: Museum Press Limited, 1961), p. 221.

[91] J. Watkins, "Antisocial Compulsions Induced Under Hypnotic Trance," *Journal of Abnormal and Social Psychology*, vol. 42, No. 2, April 1947, pp. 256-259.

[92] Marks, *The Search for the "Manchurian Candidate*, p. 195.

[93] The ability to alter a person's perceptions through hypnosis to the point of inducing him to violence in combination with the use of post-hypnotic amnesia or multiple personalities would represent an incredibly powerful weapon. A subject might very well be induced to commit murder and have no recollection of having committed the deed.

[94] In a like manner, the "programmed" right-wing personality might be used as an assassin against left wing political personalities. In either case, assuming the programmed agent were sent into the field as a spy and joined organizations or engaged in behaviors to establish credibility as a "true believer" in the appropriate political realm, these modes of behavior, in addition to allowing the agent to infiltrate and report certain organizations, could also serve as a means of establishing his credibility as a radical or extremist capable of violent behavior against members of political movements at the opposite end of the spectrum. Thus, the agent's work in the infiltration of certain political groups might also be a means of "setting him up" to take the fall for a programmed assassination attempt against members of ideologically antithetical organizations. The use of double agents in this same manner would thus provide a rationale to explain extreme behavior desired by the CIA that might be pinned on a "fall guy" operative. For instance, an apparent rabid pro-Communist would be the perfect patsy as an ideologically motivated

assassin of an anti-Communist, or the actions of the anti-Communist personality could be used to justify the assassination of a pro-Communist.

[95] Regarding the validity of Estabrooks' fantastic claims, Ross wrote: "Given the military intelligence and academic connections of Dr. Estabrooks, and the fact that all his techniques and results were achieved in real-life simulations under BLUEBIRD and ARTICHOKE, it is probable that his claims to have created and handled Manchurian Candidates during World War II are accurate and factual."

[96] Ross summarized Estabrooks' high-level connections as follows:

- "Dr. Estabrooks was accepted as a contractor by the War Department on February 20, 1942. On July 13, 1939, he received correspondence from W.S. Anderson, Director of Naval Intelligence."
- "The Estabrooks archives contain voluminous correspondence back and forth between Dr. Estabrooks and J. Edgar Hoover beginning May 13, 1936 and continuing up to March 7, 1962."
- "In an August 24, 1935 letter to Dr. Estabrooks from the Office of the Chief of Staff of the War Department, the correspondent notes communications received from Dr. Estabrooks by the Military Intelligence Division dating back to 1924."
- "Dr. Estabrooks ran a symposium for the U.S. Army Intelligence School at Fort Holabird in Baltimore on April 5-7, 1963."

[97] Ross, a psychiatrist who specialized in treating the type of trauma induced by the CIA's mind-control program, after reading 15,000 pages of declassified documents on CIA mind-control projects including MKULTRA, BLUEBIRD and ARTICHOKE concluded: "The BLUEBIRD/ARTICHOKE materials establish conclusively that full Manchurian Candidates were created and tested successfully by physicians with TOP SECRET clearance from the CIA." Ross, p. 61.

[98] This theory that Oswald was a programmed victim of the CIA with an artificially split personality exhibiting apparently conflicting traits was briefly discussed in *Operation Mind Control* by Walter Bowart. See: Bowart, *Operation Mind Control*, p. 186.

[99] Bob Callahan, *Who Shot JFK* (New York: Simon and Schuster, 1993), p. 110.

[100] Marks, *The Search for the Manchurian Candidate,* p. 196.

[101] That is, being programmed with one militantly pro-Communist personality and another militantly anti-Communist personality.

[102] Recall that this information on the application of hypnosis to espionage was published years before the Kennedy assassination took place.

[103] This research is based on an exhaustive study of newly declassified documents relative to the Kennedy assassination.

[104] For example, Oswald's mail (both in the USSR and in the U.S. after his return) was constantly intercepted and opened. This mail included correspondence with Communist and Socialist organizations. His phone calls were also monitored.

[105] As will be discussed below, Newman also proposes that Oswald, after returning from the Soviet Union, was used as a double agent in a smaller counterintelligence operation against the Cuban government and its sympathizers during his event-filled stay in New Orleans.

[106] Edward J. Epstein, *Legend: The Secret World of Lee Harvey Oswald*, (New York: McGraw-Hill Book Company, 1978), p. 117.

[107] From the questions they asked or didn't ask Oswald about the U-2 program, the CIA counterintelligence staff might determine gaps in the Soviets' knowledge regarding the program. Additionally, this information could be used to tell if the Soviets had a highly placed mole in the U.S. intelligence apparatus and, if so, where it might be located.

[108] By one estimate, 90% of U.S. intelligence on the Soviets came from the U-2 missions. The phenomenally successful U-2s carried sophisticated cameras that were reportedly capable of resolving a golf ball from 70,000 feet. Such capabilities allowed the U.S. to gain much information on the Soviets' weapons production and deployment programs, troop movements and nuclear tests. Epstein, p. 119.

[109] Philip H. Melanson, *Spy Saga: Lee Harvey Oswald and U.S. Intelligence*, (New York: Praeger, 1990), p. 18.

[110] Ibid., p. 27.

[111] The Soviets accomplished this feat shortly after Oswald's defection without any apparent breakthroughs in the relevant missile or guidance technology. Prior to this, the Soviets were unable to even accurately determine the altitude of the spy planes. As Edward Jay Epstein argues, Oswald may have provided the Soviets with access to sensitive information that allowed them to overcome or even capitalize on the U-2 plane's radar jamming capabilities, the key technical factor that contributed to the success of the U-2's ability to avoid Soviet countermeasures.

[112] James Risen, "U.S. Dangled Poison Secrets Before Soviets, Book Reports," *New York Times*, 3/5/00

[113] David Wise, *Cassidy's Run: The Secret Spy War Over Nerve Gas*, (New York: Random House, 2000), p. 197.

[114] Posner, p. 25.

[115] The low-level army sergeant the FBI picked for the spy detail had lived a life similar to Oswald's. As a young boy, due to the poverty and instability of his family life (his mother died when he was three and his father could not take care of him), he was left for several years at an orphanage (Oswald was put in an orphanage when he was three because his father had died and his mother could not take care of his family). Additionally, like Oswald, a high-school dropout, Cassidy joined the military and was stationed in Japan. After his stint in Japan, he returned to the U.S. and was recruited as a life-long spy to be "dangled" to the Soviets as a willing traitor. See: David Wise, *Cassidy's Run: The Secret Spy War Over Nerve Gas*, (New York: Random House, 2000), Chapter 4.

[116] Once the benefits to the CIA of Oswald's domestic pro-Communist act become apparent, it becomes increasingly easier to believe that Oswald played a similar role during his defection to the USSR.

[117] From its inception, the CIA has conducted illegal spying operations targeting U.S. citizens within the United States—even though it is supposedly forbidden to do so by U.S. law.

[118] Numerous internal CIA reports found these assertions to be completely false. Halperin, p. 11.

[119] This program would eventually result in the CIA opening files on 7,000 Americans and result in the diversion of 28 million pieces of mail as part of its "mail-opening" campaign. Melanson, p. 47.

[120] Ten political organizations were infiltrated under the guise of MERRIMAC including the Women's Strike for Peace, the Washington Peace Center, the Student Nonviolent Coordinating Committee (SNCC) and the Congress of Racial Equality (CORE). Melanson, p. 48.

[121] The CIA had a watch list of approximately 1,000 organizations as part of this program. Morton H. Halperin, "Led Astray by the CIA," *The New Republic*, June 28, 1975, p. 11.

[122] Halperin, p. 14.

[123] Ward Churchill and Jim Vander Wall, *Agents of Repression: The FBI's Secret Wars Against the Black Panther Party and the American Indian Movement*, (Boston: South End Press, 1990), p. 47.

[124] According to these authors, Army intelligence documents divulge that *one of every six* demonstrators at the tumultuous Chicago Democratic convention in 1969 were undercover operatives. Lee and Shlain also demonstrate how government informants quietly intersected with some of the most visible of the 60's era personalities. For example, the bodyguards of sixties activists Abbie Hoffman and Jerry Rubin were also reportedly government informants. Martin Lee and Bruce Shlain, *Acid Dreams: The Complete Social History of LSD: The CIA, The Sixties, and Beyond* (New York: Grove Weidenfeld, 1985), p. 224.

[125] Martin Lee and Bruce Shlain, *Acid Dreams: The Complete Social History of LSD: The CIA, The Sixties, and Beyond* (New York: Grove Weidenfeld, 1985), p. 224.

[126] As a high-level employee of the covert warfare infrastructure working closely with the CIA and the Joint Chiefs of Staff, Prouty's history of how the Vietnam conflict was deliberately engineered through covert operations on a grand scale is a must-read. See chapter entitled "Why Vietnam" in his 1992 book *JFK. The CIA, Vietnam and the Plot to Assassinate John F. Kennedy* (New York: Carol Publishing Group, 1992).

[127] Interestingly, as a result of the *New York Times* publishing the story in 1974 of the "massive" illegal domestic spying operation on U.S. citizens (including members of Congress), the reporter who broke the story and the *New York Times* itself were both attacked by the establishment (including other establishment media outlets). This censoring effort represented what one informed observer described as "a massive illegal domestic CIA campaign to discredit the…story." [Halperin] The reasons for this curious attempt on the part of the supposedly "watch-dog" post-Watergate press establishment to destroy persons informing the public about illegal

CIA activities have been discussed by several authors and are discussed in APPENDIX A of this study. (See the cited works of Leslie H. Gelb, Morton H. Halperin and Kathryn Olmsted.) Morton H. Halperin, "Led Astray by the CIA," *The New Republic*, June 28, 1975, p. 9.

[128] Posner, p. 209.

[129] Posner, p. 209.

[130] Like much of correspondence with Communist organizations, this letter was covertly intercepted by the FBI. Newman, p. 303.

[131] Newman, p. 306.

[132] Newman, p. 307.

[133] Ibid., pp. 243-4.

[134] Interestingly, it was through these two agents (after they met with Castro within days of the Kennedy assassination) that the FBI supposedly learned that Castro had believed that Oswald was a dangerous provocateur because he had offered to kill JFK during his pre-assassination visit to the Cuban embassy in Mexico City. Daniel Schorr, "A Conspiracy of Silences," *The New Leader*, Nov. 15-29, 1993, p. 4.

[135] Quoted in Melanson, p. 49.

[136] Halperin, p. 14.

[137] Although the CHAOS and MERRIMAC programs did not formally exist at the time of Oswald's actions, the CIA could have been using Oswald for similar purposes in preliminary operations that were ongoing at the time. In fact, Oswald's actions and his reputation as a communist sympathizer may have been used to justify the creation of these programs to root out alleged communist activity in American politics. Perhaps many of the organizations that were eventually targeted by the CIA were in fact targeted due to the "discrediting" activities of intelligence operatives and bogus leftists in the preceding years. This would not be without precedent. For example, after describing how the FBI successfully infiltrated the leadership positions of leftist organizations such as the Socialist Workers Party and the Young Socialist Alliance in the same era, Churchill and Vander Wall noted how FBI informants "thus participated in shaping the very organizational policies which the Bureau claimed it was necessary to investigate." Ward Churchill and Jim Vander Wall, *Agents of Repression: The FBI's Secret Wars Against the Black Panther Party and the American Indian Movement*, (Boston: South End Press, 1990), p. 47.

[138] See Melanson, p. 59.

[139] As part of a *New York Times* exposé on these CIA domestic spying operations, an article on January 4, 1975, revealed that from 1960 to 1970 the CIA had employed a large group of Cuban exiles to spy on suspected pro-Castro Cubans within the U.S. as well as on Americans who associated with them. The *Times* also revealed that: "Such operations reportedly directed by the intelligence agency were reportedly carried out with the knowledge and consent of the Federal Bureau of Investigation under an inter-agency agreement worked out in the wake of the Bay of Pigs invasion in 1961." George Volsky, "Cuban Exiles Recall Domestic Spying and Picketing for C.I.A.," *New York Times*, 1/4/75

[140] Another *Times* article revealed specifically that agents from the failed Bay of Pigs anti-Castro operation were recruited for these types of operations within the U.S. In a 1974 interview with the *New York Times*, E. Howard Hunt admitted to heading up the Domestic Operations Division of the CIA, the agency that oversaw much of the infiltration of American anti-war groups. Although he denies personal knowledge of these activities, Hunt reported (according to the *Times*) that the domestic unit involved in these illegal domestic activities was staffed by anti-Cuban operatives and that the operation was active at the time Oswald was in New Orleans as it "was assembled shortly after the failure of the Bay of Pigs operations in late 1961." In addition to implicating anti-Cuban operatives in the domestic surveillance program, Hunt's testimony suggests a longer-running program than is commonly admitted to by the CIA. According to the *Times*, Hunt's statements "suggest that questionable domestic activities by the CIA had apparently begun under the Kennedy Administration, continued during the Johnson Administration and…reached a peak during the antiwar outbursts in opposition to President Nixon's Vietnam policy." Seymour Hersh, "Hunt Tells of Early Work For a C.I.A. Domestic Unit," *New York Times*, 12/31/74

[141] A highly classified report (declassified in early 1998) produced by the CIA in October 1961 as the result of an internal investigation into the reasons for the Bay of Pigs failure, found that the CIA itself was to blame for the fiasco, not Kennedy. Craig Nelson, "CIA Declassifies Bay of Pigs Report," *Associated Press News Service*, February 23, 1998.

[142] One of the CIA's anti-Castro paramilitary groups, the Student Revolutionary Directorate (DRE), had to be shut down after it was infiltrated by Cuban intelligence in 1962. Newman, p. 325.

[143] This effort continues to this day. For example, the FBI recently uncovered a Cuban spy ring that was attempting to infiltrate anti-Castro groups composed of Cuban exiles in the U.S. See: Sue Anne Pressley, "10 Arrested On Charges Of Spying For Cuba, Military Facilities Targeted, FBI Alleges," *Washington Post*, 9/15/98; Patricia Zengerle, "Ten Cubans Charged With Spying On U.S. Military," *Reuters*, 9/14/98.

[144] In addition to 20 years of work with the FBI (in Chicago no-less), Banister had worked with Naval intelligence during World War II. Newman, *Oswald And The CIA*, p. 289.

[145] According to Warren Hinckle and William Turner in their study *Deadly Secrets*, Banister bragged that he had the largest database of "anti-Communist intelligence" in the South. Banister regularly shared the information in his files with New Orleans FBI. Warren Hinckle and William Turner, *Deadly Secrets*, p. 230.

[146] According to reports in the *New York Times*, in spite of efforts to stop them, Cuban agents had infiltrated U.S.-based anti-Castro operations to an amazingly successful extent. As *Times* reporter Tim Weiner recently related: "Cuba's spy service has infiltrated the exile groups of Miami for more than 30 years, compromising and sometimes controlling their work. The chief of operations of one of the most militant groups secretly reported to Fidel Castro for a decade. Dozens of

Cubans recruited by the C.I.A. during the cold war were double agents in the pay of Havana and Moscow. Some may still be." See: Tim Weiner, "Castro's Moles Dig Deep, Not Just Into Exiles," *New York Times*, 3/1/96

[147] As Newman notes: "It is possible that Banister was using Oswald to smoke out pro-Castro Cuban students in local universities and to discredit local leftwing or communist academics." Newman, *Oswald And The CIA*, p. 309.

[148] Melanson, p. 61.

[149] Hinckle and Turner, *Deadly Secrets*, p. 234.

[150] Ibid., p. 235. It should be noted that the reliability of Roberts' testimony has been called into question by the House Select Committee on Assassinations and Gerald Posner in *Case Closed*.

[151] It is possible that the domestic counterintelligence operations against American dissidents took place in two stages—the first being the infiltration of bogus leftists into legitimate left-wing organizations, the second being the use of these bogus leftists as an excuse to conduct massive surveillance and disruption of these groups. Although it is the second wave which took place during the height of the Vietnam war that got widely publicized after Seymour Hersh's front page *New York Times* exposé, it was reported by the *New York Times* within the same month of Hersh's block-buster story that the CIA had been conducting such operations from the very early '60s. Moreover, operatives such as E. Howard Hunt (who trained the Bay of Pigs paramilitary groups in Guatemala) were part of this operation. Was Oswald being used as part of this first wave to justify a massive follow up wave?

[152] As Melanson summarized: "Oswald used the show to set up the FPCC for a political and public relations disaster." Melanson, p. 68.

[153] With respect to this confrontation between Oswald and the anti-Castro activist Bringuier (whom Newman refers to as the "the Cuban with the best connections to the CIA in New Orleans"), a New Orleans police lieutenant testified that Oswald "seemed to have set them up, so to speak, to create an incident, but when the incident occurred he remained absolutely peaceful and gentle." Melanson, pp. 327, 328.

[154] As Melanson observed "Oswald's activities regarding the FPCC and the ACLU manifest a striking similarity to each other and to the CIA's worldview and modus operandi concerning domestic spying. If we reexamine his FPCC involvement from this perspective, we find an artificially created paper trail leading to the American Communist Party, similar to one he would create for the ACLU." Melanson, p. 60.

[155] See full text of the letter in Melanson, p. 71.

[156] Of this incriminating letter, Melanson writes: "It is an incredible letter, offering up a scenario that would confirm the worst paranoia of zealous anti-communists: a former Soviet defector using a pro-Castro group as a front for advancing communist ideals is unmasked, then writes his comrades in the American Communist Party to ask whether or not he should go underground. Here is proof that the insidious tentacles of Kremlin subversion reached into domestic politics in the United States, proof that the Kremlin, Castro, and the American Communist Party were linked in political action as well as ideological affinity." Melanson, p. 72.

[157] Newman, p. 345.

[158] Newman, *Oswald And The CIA*, p. 351.

[159] "In order to obtain access to foreign circles, the Agency also recruited or inserted about a dozen individuals into American dissident circles in order to establish their credentials for operations abroad." Colby quoted in: Leslie H. Gelb, "The CIA and the Press: Bearing Out Seymour Hersh," *The New Republic*, March 22, 1975, p. 13.

[160] With respect to the "Oswald-as-infiltrator" thesis, it is curious that, while he was setting up his local FPCC office, both the FBI and the CIA were intercepting Oswald's mail to the FPCC. It is also known that the CIA had spies planted in the FPCC. Was Oswald one of them? Newman, pp. 274, 5.

[161] In order to keep their sources secret, the CIA compartmentalized Oswald's files and denied past congressional investigatory access to many important documents.

[162] As mentioned previously, some researchers have argued that the Kennedy assassination was itself an act designed to provide a rationale for invading Cuba and eliminating Castro. By having an established Communist sympathizer with apparent ties to pro-Castro organizations assassinate Kennedy, the CIA might be able to accuse Oswald of being a paid Cuban agent acting on orders from Castro—thereby justifying military retaliation. This theory is more intriguing in light of the CIA memo quoted earlier in which it was proposed that a mind-controlled assassin might trigger a "bigger project." The quote in full read: "*As a 'trigger mechanism,' for a bigger project*, it was proposed that an individual, of (deleted) descent, approximately 35 years old, well educated, proficient in English and well established socially and politically in the (deleted) government *be induced under Artichoke to perform an act, involuntarily, against a prominent (deleted) politician or if necessary, against an American official.*" [emphasis added]

[163] A terminal experiment is one that ends in the death of one of the subjects of the experiment.

[164] Note how this description of the use of hypnosis to create unwitting double agents (written by Marks many years after the assassination based on declassified data) closely matches that of Estabrooks that was written well before such documents became available through the Freedom of Information Act.

[165] In light of Oswald's provocative New Orleans behavior, Estabrooks' detailed description of an apparently pro-Communist but, in actuality, a hypnotized anti-Communist agent is illuminating. As Estabrooks described, "This individual will become a rabid communist. He will join the party, follow the party line and make himself as objectionable as possible to the authorities. Note that he will be acting in good faith. He is a Communist, or rather his PA is a Communist and will behave as such." Under the model for programming a spy described by Estabrooks, Oswald's New Orleans behavior would have been under his "PA" or "Personality A" mode.

[166] Just prior to this *pro-Castro* posturing on a street corner in New Orleans, Oswald had offered his expertise as an ex-Marine to train troops for an *anti-Castro* military exercise, or if necessary, to go himself. Donald Jackson, "The Evolution of an Assassin," *Life*, February 21, 1964, p. 76.

¹⁶⁷ Recall Marks' description of the CIA mind control experiment: "Then Agency officials would tip off the local police that the man was a dangerous Communist agent, and he would be arrested."
¹⁶⁸ Donald Jackson, "The Evolution of an Assassin," *Life*, February 21, 1964, p. 76.
¹⁶⁹ As noted by Marks: "An ARTICHOKE team was scheduled to carry out field tests along these lines in the summer of 1954. The planning got to an advanced stage, with the ARTICHOKE command center in Washington cabling overseas for the 'time, place and bodies available for terminal experiments.' …At this point, the available record becomes very fuzzy…"
¹⁷⁰ If Oswald was the subject of a terminal experiment in Dallas similar to that outlined in declassified CIA memos, the fact that the mayor of Dallas, Earle Cabell, was the brother of CIA deputy director Charles Cabell (whom Kennedy had fired) would make his post-arrest questioning by "friendly" government officials and his subsequent disposal even easier.
¹⁷¹ Washington insiders such as Fletcher Prouty who were intimately involved in planning covert operations at the highest levels of the U.S. government have claimed that Kennedy was in the process of reorganizing the command structure that oversaw U.S. covert operations. Kennedy had demanded the resignation of super-spy and CIA chief Allen Dulles, as well as his deputy director Charles Cabell (whose brother was the mayor of Dallas) over the Bay of Pigs debacle. (According to Jim Garrison, it was Charles Cabell who planned the Bay of Pigs invasion.) In 1992, Prouty accurately described how Allen Dulles had unjustly blamed Kennedy for the failure of the coup attempt to shift the blame from his own agency the CIA. This was borne out in 1998, when the CIA declassified its own report on the operation. See L. Fletcher Prouty, *JFK. The CIA, Vietnam and the Plot to Assassinate John F. Kennedy* (New York: Carol Publishing Group, 1992), especially Chapter Fourteen "JFK Makes His Move to Control the CIA; Craig Nelson, "CIA Declassifies Bay of Pigs Report," *Associated Press News Service*, February 23, 1998."
¹⁷² As Newman observed: "The Oswald we watch through the eyes of the FBI agents who tracked him down—and through the eyes of the CIA personnel who read the FBI reports—looks like a would-be double agent caught in a web of intrigue far stickier than he had anticipated. Again, whether Oswald's actions were his own or the result of direction or manipulation, by carrying out both pro-Castro and anti-Castro activities in New Orleans, Oswald was playing a dangerous game." Newman, p. 318.
¹⁷³ Oswald engaged in provocative behavior for a U.S. Marine. For example, he liked to converse with his fellow Marines in Russian and insisted on using the red pieces in board games. For these actions and others, they nicknamed him "Oswaldovich."
¹⁷⁴ Interestingly, Oswald's mother Marguerite told the Warren Commission that "she believes her son went to Russia and returned as an undercover agent for the U.S. Government." (See: *The Report of the President's Commission on the Assassination of President John F. Kennedy*, p. 326.) Marguerite also confronted Lee after his redefection to the U.S. and threatened to write a book on his "so-called" defection.

This threat reportedly panicked him greatly. See: Edward J. Epstein, *Legend: The Secret World of Lee Harvey Oswald,* (New York: McGraw-Hill Book Company, 1978), p. 162.

[175] Oswald "worked" for the Reilly Coffee Company while in New Orleans. This company was managed by an ex-FBI agent and was only a block from 544 Camp Street–the location of the "front" office of another ex-FBI agent (Guy Banister) for whom Oswald may have worked (recall that Oswald had this address stamped on his political literature). *Deadly Secrets*, p. 235.

[176] These forged ID cards, displaying the name Aleck Hidell, were allegedly created by Oswald while he worked as a photo-print trainee at Jaggars-Chiles-Stoval, a Dallas-based company that did classified work for the Army Map Service (which, curiously enough, processed photos from spy planes such as those Oswald was trained to track while in the Marines). (See Epstein, pp. 192, 193.) This was a curious job for an individual with openly Communist sympathies, let alone for a former U-2 marine radar technician who had defected to the Soviet Union and offered to give up military secrets. At this employer, Oswald learned to use sophisticated photo processing equipment. In addition to his ID cards, it is thought that Oswald also processed the famous "backyard photos" at Jaggars-Chiles-Stoval. In these incriminating photos, Oswald is documented holding copies of the *Militant* (the Socialist Workers party newspaper) and the *Worker* (the Communist party newspaper), as well as the murder weapon in the Kennedy assassination. (Oswald had sent both of these papers samples of his work completed at Jaggars while offering his services to them. The issue of the *Militant* he was holding in the backyard photos contained a letter he had written to the paper.) His difficult personality aggravating his coworkers and his work deteriorating, Oswald was eventually fired from his job at Jaggars after being caught reading a Russian newspaper in the cafeteria.

[177] "The Report of the President's Commission on the Assassination of President John F. Kennedy," p. 121.

[178] The Warren Commission claimed that Oswald's FPFC Chapter was not a legitimate one. See: "The Report of the President's Commission on the Assassination of President John F. Kennedy," p. 407.

[179] Posner, pp. 204-206.

[180] The purchase of the rifle by an "alter" personality unknown to the "core" Oswald might explain how Lee could have sincerely denied having owned or ordered the rifle when in fact he had.

[181] Although the Attorney General and other government officials knew there had been previous assassination plots with the underworld, none of the testimony or documents received by the Warren Commission mentioned the CIA's assassination plots. As one congressional committee discovered: "Neither the CIA nor the FBI told the Warren Commission about the CIA attempts to assassinate Fidel Castro. Allen Dulles, former Director of Central Intelligence, was a member of the Warren Commission and presumably knew about CIA plots during his tenure with the Agency. FBI Director Hoover and senior FBI officials also knew about these earlier

plots. In July 1964, two months before the Warren Commission issued its 26-volume report of its investigation and findings, FBI officials learned that a Cuban official …was plotting with the CIA to assassinate Castro. However, there is no evidence this knowledge affected the FBI investigation of the President's assassination in any way." "The Investigation of the Assassination of President John F. Kennedy: Performance of the Intelligence Agencies," Book V, *Final Report Of The Select Committee To Study Governmental Operations With Respect To Intelligence Activities, United States Senate*, April 23, 1976, p. 5.

[182] Interestingly, Oswald had links to the Mafia as well as to anti-Castro forces. According to G. Robert Blakey, the Chief Counsel and Staff Director of the House Select Committee on Assassinations (and previously special prosecutor in the Justice Department under Robert Kennedy during the Mafia investigations), Oswald's Uncle Dutz, with whom he lived during his New Orleans stay just prior to the assassination, had ties to the Carlos Marcello Mafia organization in New Orleans (as a bookie). Oswald's mother, Marguerite, also had numerous personal ties to powerful Marcello-based underworld figures. See: Blakey and Billings, *Fatal Hour*, pp. 370-3.

[183] As one government report cryptically noted: "Although Oswald had been in contact with pro-Castro and anti-Castro groups for many months before the assassination, the CIA did not conduct a thorough investigation of questions of Cuban Government or Cuban exile involvement in the assassination." "The Investigation of the Assassination of President John F. Kennedy: Performance of the Intelligence Agencies," Book V, *Final Report Of The Select Committee To Study Governmental Operations With Respect To Intelligence Activities, United States Senate*, April 23, 1976, p. 5.

[184] T. Weiner, "Papers on Kennedy Assassination Are Unsealed, and '63 Is Revisited," *New York Times*, 8/24/93

[185] At least one high-level government investigator has broken ranks and revealed the Warren Commission's willful error in portraying Oswald as a lone nut. G. Robert Blakey, the Chief Counsel for the House Select Committee on Assassinations, described the findings of his commission in a book written after the investigation as follows: "The Commission portrayed Oswald as essentially a loner, but the evidence of his activities in New Orleans in the summer of 1963, evidence the Commission had access to, contradicted that portrayal." Blakey went even further and stated: "There were, therefore, the elements of the conspiracy in New Orleans: knowledge of an expected presidential trip to Texas; a violence-prone, pro-Castro Oswald; and an alliance of anti-Castro and underworld figures whose common bond was a hatred of the U.S. President. We came to believe that these were the elements that matured into the conspiracy that succeeded in November." Blakey and Billings, p. 394.

[186] John Newman's research also reveals that the CIA has consistently misled Congress both about the extent of its surveillance of Oswald and his wife (both in the Soviet Union and in the United States) and its detailed knowledge of Oswald's pre-assassination activities. For example, the CIA had intercepted letters to Oswald

in the Soviet Union from his mother. Once he returned to the States, the CIA illegally intercepted numerous letters Oswald wrote to various left wing organizations–including the Soviet embassy and the Fair Play for Cuba Committee (FPCC). They also intercepted and monitored Marina's letters to the Soviet embassy in the U.S. as well as letters to Marina from the Soviet Union. In addition to the monitoring of the Oswalds' personal mail, they monitored numerous telephone calls Lee made–including those to the Cuban embassy on his infamous trip to Mexico City shortly before the Kennedy assassination. The level of interest Oswald generated at the highest levels of the CIA certainly bears further investigation. (For example, Oswald was placed on an exclusive list of only 300 people whose mail was to be illegally intercepted and monitored by the CIA.)

[187] Documents released by the CIA show that Oswald was being tracked by the FBI through informants and interviews for three years prior to the assassination. "World Wide: The CIA," *Wall Street Journal*, 5/13/92

[188] Perhaps Oswald, like the secretary described by Marks used in Morse Allen's experiments, committed the murder while in a hypnotically induced trance and awoke from the trance denying that he had or was even capable of killing anyone. This would allow Oswald to be sincere in his denials of being the Presidential assassin even though he had indeed pulled the trigger.

[189] During a visit to the Cuban Consulate on this same Mexico City trip, Oswald was reportedly overheard threatening to kill President Kennedy. Although the accuracy of this report has been debated, it was reported to the Warren Commission by FBI director at the time, J. Edgar Hoover. Clarence Kelly, who succeeded Hoover, believed in the veracity of this report. See: Newman, pp. 428, 429.

[190] This activity may have been tied to a CIA plan to blame the Soviets or Cubans for the murder of JFK, in case the Oswald-as-lone-nut scenario fell through.

[191] Newman, p. 429.

[192] Marks, *The Search For The Manchurian Candidate*, p. 197.

[193] As a Senate Intelligence Committee noted "CIA's Cuban operations had created an enormous Domestic apparatus which the Agency used both to gather intelligence domestically and to run operations against Cuba." Senate Select Committee to Study Governmental Operations, 1976, quoted in *Deadly Secrets*, p. 268.

[194] Alan Weberman and Michael Canfield link H. L. Hunt of Watergate fame to the Kennedy assassination in their study *Coup D' État: The CIA and the Assassination of John F. Kennedy* (San Francisco: Quick American Archives, 1992).

[195] Howard Baker, the vice chairman of the Senate Watergate committee, and the minority counsel were convinced that the Watergate break-in was merely another component of the CIA's illegal domestic surveillance activities. E. Howard Hunt, who was convicted for his role in the Watergate break-ins admitted that he had conducted similar operations for the LBJ Whitehouse against the Barry Goldwater campaign. (Hunt was also heavily involved in the CIA's anti-Castro operations.) See: Seymour Hersh, "Baker Asks New Inquiry On C.I.A.-Watergate Links," *New York Times*, 1/5/75, Seymour Hersh, "Hunt Tells of Early Work For a C.I.A. Domestic Unit," *New York Times*, 12/31/96

[196] *Deadly Secrets*, p. 16.

[197] Thus, Lee Harvey Oswald and the Kennedy assassination may have been merely one particular episode in which this group played an active role in altering the path of American history. The anti-Castro Cubans may have ended the Presidency of John Kennedy as well as Richard Nixon (through the Watergate scandal). Was Oswald merely a symptom of more widespread disease?

[198] "The Strange Tale of Dr. Narut," *The Sunday Times*, 7/6/75

[199] Narut's work involved teaching combat readiness units "to cope with the stress of killing."

[200] In the course of the astonishing interview with the *Times* reporter, Dr. Narut also stated that psychological tests such as the Minnesota Multiphasic Personality Inventory (or MMPI) were used to pre-select future killers for this training. Perhaps similar testing was used to ease the difficulties described by Estabrooks associated with finding enough highly suggestive persons for service in an organization of hypno-programmed operatives and spies. As Estabrooks noted:

"Finally, we again point out that we are fully aware of the difficulties which would be encountered in building up such an organization. Hardly one somnambulist in, say, ten, or even one hundred, would be suitable for such work; and the determining of this suitability would be no easy task. But it could be done, and once accomplished would repay amply all the trouble."

[201] Interestingly enough, as a boy, Oswald was diagnosed by a psychiatrist as having a "cold, detached outer attitude" and as having "schizoid features and passive-aggressive tendencies." Posner, p. 13.

[202] Epstein, p. 66.

[203] One of Oswald's fellow marines noted that Oswald changed after his stay at Atsugi: "He had started to be more aggressive…he took on a new personality, and now he was Oswald the man rather than Oswald the rabbit." Posner, p. 26.

[204] According to Ross: "Dr. Estabrooks was accepted as a contractor by the War Department on February 20, 1942. On July 13, 1939, he received correspondence from W.S. Anderson, Director of Naval Intelligence." Ross, p. 172. Guy Banister also had connections to Naval Intelligence.

[205] In addition to describing how split personality could be induced to create spies to infiltrate communist groups, Estabrooks wrote in detail of how the same technique could be used to create spies to infiltrate fascist and Nazi groups. In one case, he reviewed how he could turn a normal man into a "perfect spy" with extremely polarized values by inducing multiple personalities through hypnosis:

"If we had tried this trick in World War II, we would have found ourselves a young man of unimpeachable patriotism and high suggestibility, and, in order to make him into a perfect spy, we would then have deliberately produced a split personality in him. We would, further, have *so constructed this Dr. Jekyll and Mr. Hyde* that the primary personality—that is, the conscious personality, the personality with which the subject identified himself—became everything he had previously abhorred." [emphasis added]

Estabrooks then went on to sarcastically describe exactly how he could completely reverse and destroy the personality of his perfect spy through "kindly ministrations" to convert him into a raving Nazi Storm Trooper:

"Before we begin to work on him, our subject is a…man of democratic principles, to whom all the brutality and race-hatred of Nazism are repugnant beyond words; a man who firmly believes that all men are created equal, a man who firmly believes that aggressive war should not be an instrument of national policy; a man to whom freedom and liberty are as precious as life. *After a few months or our kindly ministrations he emerges somewhat altered. Now he is anti-Semitic, antidemocratic, antiegalitarian, antilibertarian, sadistic, warlike—perfect Storm Trooper material.*" [emphasis added]

Estabrooks notes that this new man could be useful to infiltrate the Nazi party and even potentially rise to a position of importance in the organization:

"And believing, as he now does,…he runs out and joins his local branch of the Nazi Bund and throws himself enthusiastically into all its activities. With his energy, vigor, and conviction, he may even rise to a position of some importance in the organization. Now he is a dedicated Nazi, an enemy to everything his country stands for."

Estabrooks then described how American counterintelligence agents could tap into the programmed secondary personality through a posthypnotic cue to spy on targeted groups: "the good little Nazi, immediately falls into deep trance, becomes a loyal American once again, and reveals all the little Nazi plans he and his playmates have made during the week." George H. Estabrooks and Nancy E. Gross, *The Future of the Human Mind*, (London: Museum Press Limited, 1961), p. 222.

[206] Estabrooks bragged: "It worked beautifully for months…"

[207] George Estabrooks, "Hypnosis Comes of Age," *Science Digest*, April, 1971, pp. 44-50, reprinted in Ross, pp. 167-170.

[208] Oswald dated women from one exclusive nightclub called the Queen Bee (which was known for its exquisitely beautiful female hostesses) where a single evening could easily have cost him a month's salary. The ability to maintain this lifestyle is consistent with his having disposable income from powerful friends.

[209] In a 1983 *Rolling Stone* article, Martin Lee, Robert Ranftel and Jeff Cohen discuss Oswald's possible involvement in American LSD experiments conducted at Atsugi. They quote another ex-Marine who was stationed at Atsugi as stating: "It was pretty weird…I'm eighteen and chasing all the whores in town, and these CIA guys are buying my drinks and paying for the whores and giving me a whole lot of

drinks with lots of weird drugs in them." See: M. Lee, R. Ranftel and J. Cohen, "Did Lee Harvey Oswald Drop Acid?" *Rolling Stone*, March 3, 1983, pp. 20-54.

[210] George Estabrooks, "Hypnosis Comes of Age," reprinted in Ross, pp. 167-170.

[211] Some of these hostesses were known to be informants for foreign intelligence agencies. Posner, p. 25.

[212] Epstein, pp. 82, 83.

[213] Epstein, p. 71, Posner, p. 24.

[214] Ferrie has been accused of using his passion for hypnosis as a means of luring men and boys into homosexual liaisons. Bowart, *Operation Mind Control*, p. 193.

[215] Bowart, *Operation Mind Control*, p. 193.

[216] Ibid., p. 193.

[217] It is possible that Oswald was recruited for such activities much earlier than is suspected by many researchers. Scientists studying hypnosis developed numerous tests to determine whether a person would be readily susceptible to hypnosis. By making correlations between measured hypnotic susceptibility and other psychiatric factors, scientists determined that adults who had been abused as children were especially susceptible to hypnosis. [M. Nash, S. Lynn, D. Givens, "Adult Hypnotic Susceptibility, Childhood Punishment, and Child Abuse: A Brief Communication," *The International Journal of Clinical and Experimental Hypnosis*, 1984, vol. XXXII, No. 1, pp. 6-11.] Although beyond the scope of this study, it might be fruitful to investigate whether Oswald was given such tests and at what age he was recruited (assuming the thesis of this study is true) by the CIA. Perhaps Oswald (who led an abusive childhood) was one of the children recruited for mind control studies by the CIA as described in recent testimony before the Presidential Advisory Committee On Human Radiation Experiments investigating government radiation experimentation on U.S. citizens. (This investigative body heard testimony that children were often victims of CIA mind control studies. In addition to serving as human guinea pigs for experimentation, it is alleged that these children are also used in CIA-backed child pornography rings to blackmail prominent politicians as a means of controlling their behavior.) See also: *Operation Mind Control*, Freedom of Thought Foundation, Limited Researcher's Edition, (#131), 1995, PO Box 35072, Tucson, AZ 85740-5072

[218] Melanson, p. 43.

[219] Tom Squitieri, "JFK Files May Shed Light on Witness's Death," *USA Today*, 2/20/92.

[220] Epstein, p. 182.

[221] Epstein, p. 362.

[222] Fatal Hour, p. 378.

[223] Hinckle and Turner, *Deadly Secrets*, p. 238.

[224] Paul J. Reiter, *Antisocial or Criminal Acts and Hypnosis A Case Study* (Copenhagen: Munksgaard, 1958).

[225] The criminal hypnotist, though supposedly an amateur, was also able to set up a sophisticated locking system that frustrated psychologists attempting to hypnotize the victim after his arrest during psychological treatment for the extreme neurosis

brought on by the previous hypnotic manipulation of his personality. Similar locking systems are reportedly used by the CIA to ensure that enemy intelligence agencies can't hypnotize captured spies and access their highly sensitive knowledge.

[226] In fact, Oswald and the Nazi collaborator/mind control victim described by Reiter may have had the same hypno programmers—the CIA! According to a news report published in the *London Sunday Mail*, Stephen Saracco, a New York public prosecutor investigating the suspicious death of CIA mind-control victim Dr. Frank Olson, claims the "CIA was using German SS prisoners and Norwegian quislings (collaborators) taken from jails and detention centres as guinea pigs to test [Ewen] Cameron's theories about mind control." Saracco believes the CIA was conducting "terminal" experiments (involving the deaths of the subjects) on Germans and Scandinavians. What a coincidence that the case described by Reiter involves a German soldier and a Scandinavian citizen who was programmed to engage in terminal behavior while being jailed for collaboration with the Nazis. Was the case described above, which has numerous parallels to the Kennedy assassination, the result of such CIA terminal experiments? Was this a prototype for a terminal experiment that resulted in the Kennedy assassination? See: Kevin Dowling, "Cold War Crimes Trial? The Olson File: A Secret That Could Destroy The CIA," *London Sunday Mail*, August 23, 1998.

[227] Oswald is also accused of having committed a double murder. While on the run following his alleged assassination of Kennedy he allegedly shot Dallas Police Officer J.D. Tippit after the officer stopped him on the street.

[228] If this scenario in which Oswald-the-defector is used as a hypnotically manipulated double agent and assassin is accurate, it would represent the fulfillment of similar, although unrealized, British plans targeting leaders in Nazi Germany during the closing phase of the Second World War. In this case, the British Special Operations Executive contemplated turning Hitler's deputy Rudolph Hess, a *defector* who had fled to Britain, into a hypnotically controlled double agent who could be sent back into Nazi Germany to assassinate Heinrich Himmler. Tom Kuntz, "Blow the Führer From the Train and Other British Plots," *New York Times*, 8/2/98

[229] As Chase summarized: "In the fall of 1958 Theodore Kaczynski, a brilliant but vulnerable boy of sixteen, entered Harvard College. There he encountered a prevailing intellectual atmosphere of anti-technological despair. There, also, he was deceived into subjecting himself to a series of purposely brutalizing psychological experiments—experiments that may have confirmed his still-forming belief in the evil of science." Alston Chase, "Harvard and the Making of the Unabomber," *Atlantic Monthly*, June 2000, pp. 41-65.

[230] Murray monitored brainwashing experiments in the military and developed brutal methods for determining how to break a man down through stress. He also headed up the Personality Assessments section of the OSS, the forerunner of the CIA. Murray's research involved developing stress/personality tests for determining how well a recruit could stand up to trauma. This was to provide a defensive tool that would assist the military in selecting men for missions that might involve hostile

enemy interrogation. A side-benefit of this technology was an offensive capability for destroying men through the scientific production of stress.

[231] Such methods could also be used to test the "stress inoculation" procedures the military desired to implement, which promised to make their spies impervious to enemy interrogation through hypnosis and torture. As is often the case in such endeavors, researchers had to develop the offensive capability to determine if the defense against it was viable. Similar reasoning justified the military's development of offensive biological warfare agents so they could test the feasibility of vaccines against them.

[232] As Chase wrote: "In their postwar form these experiments focused on stressful dyadic relations, designing confrontations akin to those mock interrogations he had helped to orchestrate for the OSS."

[233] These follow-up sessions would involve hundreds of hours and hundreds of pages of hand-written personal information provided by the student-subjects about themselves. Additionally, the young students were often shown the movies taken of themselves being helplessly humiliated by the experimental interrogator.

[234] As Alston Chase concisely observed: "Rather than inculcate traditional values, they sought to undermine them."

[235] Harvard educates a grotesquely disproportionate number of America's most powerful government leaders—especially those concerned with overseeing and rationalizing the national security state and its covert actions. Could the curriculum at Harvard as described by Chase represent a sophisticated mind control system for making sure that these leaders are educated and screened for amoral compliance through personality manipulation? This indoctrination system might partially explain why America's leaders have allowed the American public to be used as guinea pigs in massive, decades-long testing programs with radiation, drugs and biological warfare agents. For an excellent summary of Harvard's lopsided role in the US power structure, see: ed. John Trumpbour, *How Harvard Rules*, (Boston: South End Press, 1989), especially chapter entitled: "Harvard, the Cold War, and the National Security State," pp. 51-128.

[236] Henry Murray, the psychiatrist in charge of the experiments Kaczynski was subjected to at Harvard, had monitored CIA brainwashing experiments with truth drugs and was an enthusiastic supporter of the drug research conducted after the war at Harvard by Timothy Leary, et. al.

[237] After his return to Harvard after the war, Morris apparently continued his research for the military. One of the grant applications he filled out proposed "the development of a system of procedures for testing the suitability of officer candidates for the navy."

[238] "The educational system continues to promote bleak visions of the future. Meanwhile, alienating ideologies, offering the false promise of quick solutions through violence, proliferate."

[239] Experiments and precedents were described earlier in which subjects were hypnotized and convinced that they faced dire consequences if they did not act in an extreme manner. In some cases, subjects were convinced to form underground

political movements to fight their cause for society at-large. In other cases, murderous actions were achieved as a result of hypnotic sessions in which the subject had his perceptions of reality warped to the point he thought he was in a life-or-death struggle and that lethal force was therefore justifiable. In light of these cases, and Kacznyski's treatment and subsequent actions, it is natural to wonder what exactly happened to Kaczynski and his fellow guinea pig students at the hands of Harvard's CIA psychologist. Were they given similar hypnotic or pharmacological treatments to depattern them and destroy their personalities? (Martin Lee and Bruce Shlain reported: "The powerful ego-shattering effects of LSD were ideally suited for this purpose.") One is also tempted to ask whether Kaczynski or his fellow students were programmed with hypnosis and/or multiple personalities for later "political" activities. Given the experimentation with personality altering drugs going on at Harvard, as well as Murray's interest in military brainwashing technology, it is also tempting to ask if Kaczynski or his fellow students were used as guinea pigs in the development of preventative treatments against such measures. After all, the military was intensely interested not only in using such extreme methods for predicting how men could be "broken" down but using this technology for inoculating them against the use of such techniques by "enemy" governments. One can easily envision controlled experiments in which some subjects were given psychological treatments designed to make them less prone to break under stress and drug-assisted interrogations while others were not. (Recall the experiment described earlier in which scientists were able to induce or reduce the intensity of the LSD experience through hypnosis.) Researchers could then evaluate the viability of their "inoculation" procedures by measuring the different response rates of the groups under the stressful personality-altering procedures.

[240] The CIA did this by creating and stage-managing media outlets (see APPENDIX A), subsidizing "leftist" intellectuals and politicians, creating political and artistic trends and manipulating controlled "critics" on a global scale.

[241] Laurence Zuckerman, "How the CIA Played Dirty Tricks With Culture," *New York Times*, 3/18/00

[242] Much like the doctors who did compartmentalized research for the CIA under the MKULTRA program, many of the artists and intellectuals that were working on CIA "culture projects" were not even aware that the CIA was the source of their funding.

[243] Laurence Zuckerman, "How the CIA Played Dirty Tricks With Culture," *New York Times*, 3/18/00

[244] Frances Stonor Saunders, *The Cultural Cold War: The CIA And The World of Arts and Letters*, (New York: The New Press, 1999), p. 291.

[245] Saunders, p. 459.

[246] Saunders, p. 289.

[247] For example, following his death, CIA operatives secured the rights to George Orwell's *Animal Farm* from his widow. The CIA financed the production and international distribution of an animated version of the book while changing the ending to suit its anti-Communist propaganda goals. The CIA also changed the

movie version ending of Orwell's *1984* for similar reasons. The CIA even had favorable reviews printed in the U.S. newspapers to generate a positive reaction to the films. Saunders, pp. 294-298.

[248] Laurence Zuckerman, "How the CIA Played Dirty Tricks With Culture," *New York Times*, 3/18/00

[249] Saunders, p. 136.

[250] For example, C.D. Jackson, a vice-president at *Time Magazine*, was described as "one of America's leading psychological warfare specialists." He was also "a director of the United Negro College Fund, a trustee of the Boston Symphony Orchestra, and sat on the boards of the Lincoln Center for the Planning of Arts, the Metropolitan Opera Association, and the Carnegie Corporation of New York." Saunders, p. 147.

[251] The Ford Foundation was one of the wealthiest and most powerful foundations in the US. It was also one of the CIA's main assets in the Culture War. As Saunders wrote: "[T]he Ford Foundation became officially engaged as one of those organizations the CIA was able to mobilize for political warfare against Communism. The foundation's archives reveal a raft of joint projects." Much like the powerful network of foundations run by the Rockefeller brothers, the Ford Foundation had top-level links to the CIA. For example, John J. McCloy, an intimate of the Rockefeller family business empire, as President of the Ford Foundation in the 1950s set up "an administrative unit within the Ford Foundation specifically to deal with the CIA." (McCloy had worked closely with the CIA as High Commissioner of Germany following the war.) In the 1960s McGeorge Bundy became president of the Ford Foundation, "coming straight from his job as Special Assistant to the President in Charge of National Security, which meant, among other things, monitoring the CIA". There were similar interlocks between philanthropy and intelligence in the Rockefeller sphere. Nelson Rockefeller was a trustee of the powerful Rockefeller Brothers Fund in addition to being "Eisenhower's special adviser on Cold War strategy in 1954" and Chairman "of the Planning Coordination Group which oversaw all National Security Council decisions, including CIA covert operations." Saunders, pp. 141, 142, 260, 261.

[252] In addition to his powerful position at Chase Manhattan Bank, David Rockefeller was routinely briefed on CIA matters by Tom Braden with the CIA director's permission. (Saunders, p. 145) David served on other boards, which gave him broad economic, civic and cultural influence. For example, in 1967, *Newsweek* listed the "countless array of personal and family philanthropic, economic-development and investment programs" David was associated with, including: Rockefeller Center (Director); Rockefeller Brothers Fund (Vice President); Sealantic Fund (President); Rockefeller University (Chairman); Harvard College (President Board of Overseers); Museum of Modern Art (Chairman); and the Council on Foreign Relations (Vice President). Nelson Rockefeller, whose intelligence connections are detailed above, had similar connections. As he informed Congress at his nomination hearings for Vice President in 1974, Nelson had assumed "the Presidency and Chairmanship of Rockefeller Center, the Chairmanship of IBEC [International Basic

Economy Corporation] and A.I.A. [American International Association for Economic and Social Development], the Museum of Modern Art and the Rockefeller Brothers Fund."

[253] Saunders referred to this network as "an entrepreneurial coalition of philanthropic foundations, business corporations and other institutions and individuals, who worked hand in hand with the CIA to provide the cover and the funding pipeline for its secret programmes in western Europe." Saunders, p. 129.

[254] John J. McCloy, who oversaw the CIA's use of the Ford Foundation to fund its international covert activities, served on the Warren Commission investigation of the JFK assassination (alongside Allen Dulles, former head of the CIA). Nelson Rockefeller, who oversaw all CIA operations from his position at the top of the National Security Council, headed a 1970s-era government investigation into CIA assassinations and abuses (see also Appendix A).

[255] These activities allowed the CIA to manipulate groups and even national governments into leftist behavior that it could control, thus blunting independent leftist behavior that was outside of its control or allegedly under the Soviets' control. In other words, to control the "real" left, the CIA created leftist movements of its own design that would remain under its own influence.

[256] James Risen, "How a Plot Convulsed Iran in '53 (and in '79)," *New York Times*, 4/16/00

[257] Ibid.

[258] Ibid.

[259] Cuba was targeted as a result of Castro's overthrowing of a U.S.-backed dictator, his subsequent nationalization of U.S.-owned property and his close ties to the Soviet Union.

[260] The planners at the Pentagon even had contingency plans for blaming Castro, should John Glenn's historic Mercury flight into space have accidentally crashed. Tim Weiner, "A Blast at Secrecy in Kennedy Killing," *New York Times*, 9/29/98

[261] Anthony Boadle, "U.S. Weighed Provoking War with Cuba in 1963-Document," *Reuters*, January 29, 1998.

[262] Given this level of effort targeting Cuba, one wonders if Oswald's actions as a highly visible Communist sympathizer, pro-Cuban activist and alleged assassin were designed to justify an invasion of Cuba following the JFK assassination, much like violence orchestrated by the CIA through its phony Communists was used in Iran prior to the U.S. overthrow of its government. One researcher has postulated that the Kennedy assassination was indeed intended to provide a rationale for a second (post-Bay of Pigs) invasion of Cuba. Blaming the assassination on an apparently pro-Castro activist (Oswald) who was supposedly acting on orders from Castro was intended to incense the American public to the point of supporting another Cuban invasion. [See: Claudia Furiati, *ZR Rifle: The Plot To Kill Kennedy and Castro*, (Melbourne, Australia: Ocean Press, 1994), pp. 158-162.] These plans, if they existed, were not carried out by the new post-assassination President Johnson who ironically used this potentially explosive scenario as an excuse to pin the

assassination on a "lone-nut" portrayed as having no ties to Cuba (and of course none to the CIA).

[263] Stephen Engelberg, "A Haitian Leader of Paramilitaries Was Paid by C.I.A.," *New York Times*, 10/8/94

[264] Tim Weiner, "C.I.A. Spent Millions to Support Japanese Right in 50's and 60's," *New York Times*, 10/9/94

[265] Such infiltration could come in handy when the CIA needed extreme measures to impose the regime of its choice on a given nation, or transfer power from one government faction to an alleged outsider dissident faction. In the latter case, power would appear to change hands but would in fact stay in the same hands.

[266] One-time Director of Central Intelligence William Colby summarized this process before a Senate Armed Services Committee: "In order to obtain access to foreign circles, the Agency also recruited or inserted about a dozen individuals into American dissident circles in order to establish their credentials for operations abroad." Leslie H. Gelb, "The CIA and the Press: Bearing Out Seymour Hersh," *The New Republic*, March 22, 1975, p. 13.

[267] Roger Morris, *Partners in Power*, (New York: Henry Hold and Company, Inc., 1996), pp. 102-104.

[268] The CIA reportedly used its influence in obtaining draft deferments for those students who agreed to infiltrate the anti-war movement.

[269] Like Oswald, Clinton also made a mysterious trip to Russia where he lived far above his modest means as a student, staying in one of the finest hotels in Moscow.

[270] Interestingly enough, one of the locations where Oswald is suspected of engaging in domestic Cointelpro activities was in Clinton, Louisiana.

[271] "Throughout the frenzy and turmoil of the Lewinsky scandal, Clinton's famed compartmentalization was put to its strongest test. Clinton had to attend to the business of the presidency while he simultaneously dealt with a very public scandal about his private life." Nightline/Frontline documentary: "The Clinton Years," Chapter 5: Renewal/Impeachment. http://www.pbs.org/wgbh/pages/frontline/shows/clinton/; *ABC News Internet Ventures, 2000*.

[272] Marks, *The Search for the "Manchurian Candidate,"* p. 204.

[273] Oswald allegedly shot at General Walker using the same rifle he allegedly used in the Kennedy assassination. Firing through a window in the General's home (where he sat in the dining room), the assassin missed. Oswald would later attend a speech given by Walker at a right-wing gathering several months prior to the Kennedy murder. [Donald Jackson, "The Evolution of an Assassin," *Life*, February 21, 1964, p. 78.]

[274] In Richard Condon's brilliant novel the *Manchurian Candidate* (which foreshadowed the Kennedy assassination), the U.S. soldier who was programmed and conditioned to be a mind-controlled assassin (as a means of affecting U.S. presidential politics) was given the task of a warm-up assassination prior to his attempted assassination of a U.S. presidential candidate. Curiously, the victim of the character's first assassination was at the opposite end of the political spectrum of his second victim.

[275] See L. Alvarez, "A Physicist Examines the Kennedy Assassination Film," *Am. J. Phys.*, Vol. 44, No. 9, September 1976, pp. 813-827.

[276] According to Alvarez, the momentum of the material "ejected" from the president's head in the direction of the bullet's travel on impact could easily have been greater than the incoming momentum of the bullet. Thus, in order to conserve momentum in the collision, the head must move in the opposite direction (that is in the direction from which the bullet was fired). Alvarez was able to experimentally verify the kinetics of this hypothesis by shooting watermelons wrapped in tape with a high-powered rifle and watching them recoil in the direction of the shooter.

[277] As a former consultant to the company that produced the camera used by Abraham Zapruder (Bell and Howell Company), Alvarez had extensive knowledge of the camera used and the motion produced by human operators holding the camera without mechanical support. In fact, Alvarez was working on the development of camera stabilizers for hand-held cameras made by the same company that made Abraham Zapruder's camera at the time Kennedy was shot. His analysis of the film and the timing of the fired bullets were based on the neuromuscular contractions of Zapruder (which were measured based on careful analysis of the streaking in the images recorded on the developed film caused by angular accelerations of the camera) in response to the startling auditory stimuli of the fatal gunshots fired in close proximity.

[278] This estimate of the number of shots fired at Kennedy is consistent with the research of an early investigator named Josiah Thompson who conducted an exhaustive study of the testimony of the eyewitnesses at the assassination (172 of the 190 at the scene). In his study entitled *Six Seconds In Dallas*, Thompson revealed that more people reported hearing only "two shots" (12) and "two or three" shots (10) than the total number reporting hearing "three or four" (5), "four" and (6) "more than four" (3). Josiah Thompson, *Six Seconds In Dallas*, (USA: Bernard Geis Associates, 1967), p. 25.

[279] John K. Lattimer, *Kennedy and Lincoln: Medical and Ballistic Comparisons of Their Assassinations*, (New York: Harcourt Brace Jovanovich, 1980).

[280] Lattimer even used ammunition from the same batch as that used by Oswald.

[281] In addition to this empirical research that supports the single gunman theory, Lattimer argues that Oswald's rifle training (with a bolt action rifle) as a Marine sharpshooter clearly provided him with the ability to complete the assassination himself. Oswald's Marine rifle scorebooks show that he hit targets with the required precision from a much greater distance than that that existed between Kennedy and his perch in the School Book Depository. Specifically, they show that he scored 49 out of 50 points shooting rapid fire at head-and-shoulders military targets from a distance of more than twice that (200 yards) required for the assassination and *without the benefit of a scope*. See: Lattimer, *Kennedy and Lincoln*, p. 293.

[282] Through empirical analysis using the same model rifle as that used by Oswald on simulated targets, Lattimer demonstrated that the Mannlicher-Carcano rifle used by Oswald was indeed accurate enough and reliable enough to do the shooting. With a little practice, his high school aged son was even able to duplicate, on simulated

targets, the precision shooting required in roughly the same time period that would have been needed by Oswald.

[283] For a discussion of the single bullet theory, see the Warren Commission Report chapter "The Bullet Wounds," *The Report of the President's Commission on the Assassination of President John F. Kennedy*, pp. 85-117.

[284] Lattimer's argument is that the "magic" bullet was traveling at a greatly reduced velocity (having gone through Kennedy's neck) when it hit bone in Connally's body and that it hit bone at an oblique angle (due to tumbling after leaving Kennedy's body) instead of head-on. In Lattimer's model, this would account for the fact that the nose of the bullet is undeformed as well as the minimal deformation at the rear of the so-called magic bullet. As evidence showing that the single bullet could have pierced Kennedy's neck without being deformed, Lattimer reproduces pictures of bullets similar to those used by Oswald which, in tests, penetrated 25 inches of elm wood and 47 inches of ponderosa pine without being deformed. See: Lattimer, *Kennedy and Lincoln*, p. 272.

[285] In light of the arguments above, the thesis should be considered that the perpetuation of assassination conspiracy literature that attempts to absolve Oswald from all guilt in the crime of assassinating President Kennedy serves to eliminate consideration of who Oswald really was as well as to whom he was connected…and thus serves the interests of the intelligence agencies who might have "programmed" him. Perhaps persons who perpetuate this thesis are, ironically, actually wittingly or unwittingly serving to hide the CIA's true role in the assassination while appearing to blame it.

[286] George H. Estabrooks and Nancy E. Gross, *The Future of the Human Mind*, (London: Museum Press Limited, 1961), p. 226.

[287] In fact, the day Kennedy was murdered, a CIA assassin was informed of the crime as he was leaving a meeting in which a forthcoming assassination attempt on Castro was discussed.

[288] Within the same month of the Kennedy assassination, the CIA also orchestrated the assassination of President Diem of Vietnam.

[289] Allen Dulles was one of the most powerful spies in the post-war world. It was under his charge that the CIA ballooned into an organization with its own army and air force.

[290] Not only Oswald, but Jack Ruby, the man who eliminated Oswald while in police custody, had extensive links to organized crime as well as anti-Castro forces. See: Blakey and Billings, *Fatal Hour*, pp. 329-335.

[291] Recall that declassified documents indicate that the CIA was considering using trained assassinations against American officials. See: "The Investigation of the Assassination of President John F. Kennedy: Performance of the Intelligence Agencies," Book V, *Final Report Of The Select Committee To Study Governmental Operations With Respect To Intelligence Activities, United States Senate*, April 23, 1976, p. 99.

[292] As John Newman stated: "The Warren Commission's 1964 investigation into the Kennedy assassination failed to consider the CIA's anti-Castro operations in any

capacity at all. ...There could be no more profound omission to any study of Oswald's activities in the months before the murder of Kennedy than that of the CIA's anti-Cuban operations." Newman, *Oswald And The CIA*, p. 91.

[293] As Jim Garrison eloquently summarized: "In most countries, a powerful individual who had been in open conflict with a national leader who was later assassinated would receive at least a modicum of attention in the course of the posthumous inquiry. A major espionage organization with a highly sophisticated capability for accomplishing murder might receive even more. Certainly a powerful individual who also held a top position in a major espionage apparatus and had been at odds with the departed leader would be high on the list of suspects. .... However, General Cabell, who fit that description perfectly, was never even called as a witness before the Warren Commission. One reason may have been that Allen Dulles, the former CIA director (also fired by President Kennedy) was a member of the Commission and handled all leads relating to the Agency. During the nine years that Dulles had been the CIA's chief, General Charles Cabell had been his deputy." See Jim Garrison, *On the Trail of the Assassins*, (New York: Warner Books, 1988), pp. 120-21.

[294] It is curious with respect to this hypothesis that, according to his brother, Oswald's favorite television show as a youth was "I Led Three Lives for the FBI"–a show about an FBI informant who was also a spy. It is also of interest that a guest at Oswald's house reported seeing a book entitled *How to Be a Spy*, on the Oswald's coffee table. [Gerald Posner, *Case Closed*, pp. 90-92.] An added curiosity is the caption to a photo of Oswald with a female classmate in the yearbook of the Arlington Heights High School he attended in Fort Worth, Texas. The caption to the photo in which the classmate jokingly points a finger at Oswald read: "Bing! You're Hypnotized." Lattimer, p. 125.

[295] In light of JFK's complicity in these anti-Castro operations through Operation Mongoose, this theory has been labeled the "Cuban boomerang" by some researchers. That is, that the paramilitary strike force set up by the Kennedy brothers to get Castro (called Operation Mongoose) backfired and killed JFK.

[296] Some of these curious anomalies were summarized by John Newman as follows: "As Oswald engaged in pro-Castro and anti-Castro activities, the FBI says they lost track of him. The Army was monitoring his activities and says it destroyed their reports. The record of his propaganda operations in New Orleans published by the Warren Commission turned out to have been deliberately falsified. A surprising number the [sic] characters in Oswald's New Orleans episode turned out to be informants or contract agents of the CIA." Newman, *Oswald And The CIA*, p. 427.

[297] This investigation might also include a re-opening of the investigation into the extensive links between the CIA and the mass media that were uncovered by the Church committee (only to quashed by then-CIA director George Bush). Such collusion between the elite press and the CIA (see Appendix A) would explain how Oswald's numerous connections to the CIA have gone unreported for such a long time.

[298] Fresh from its successful overthrow of the democratically elected government of Iran in 1953, the U.S. used the same "blueprint" of psychological warfare and violence *in the Western Hemisphere* to overthrow the democratically elected government of Guatemala in 1954. Moving ever closer to the U.S., CIA personnel associated with the Guatemalan coup began training to overthrow the government of Cuba in 1962. When this mission failed at the Bay of Pigs, the CIA wrongly blamed Kennedy. Personnel associated with these CIA psychological warfare and paramilitary efforts were illegally operating in the U.S. at the time of the JFK assassination.

[299] Lieutenant Colonel Prouty was the "senior Air Force officer responsible for the provision of military support of the clandestine activities of the CIA" during the early cold war days. (Prouty blames the CIA for Kennedy's assassination, but not Oswald.) L. Fletcher Prouty, *JFK. The CIA, Vietnam and the Plot to Assassinate John F. Kennedy* (New York: Carol Publishing Group, 1992), p. 82.

[300] Tim Weiner, "C.I.A. Director Admits to Failure In Disclosing Links to Guatemala," *New York Times*, 4/6/95

[301] Eric Schmitt, "School for Assassins, or Aid to Latin Democracy?" *New York Times*, 4/3/95

[302] See APPENDIX A for an analysis of why the establishment press in the U.S. has refused to cover such CIA crimes to any great extent.

[303] An investigation to this end should include an extensive and thorough review of withheld CIA documents as well as reports involving the surveillance of Oswald that still remain classified today. The Warren Commission completely ignored these documents and the House Select Committee on Assassination was prevented from seeing many of the files. (Many of those that they did see are still classified.)

[304] Lyndon Johnson, 1973 quoted in L. Janos, "The Last Days of the President," *Atlantic Monthly*, July 1973, pp. 35-41.

[305] This manipulation is so extensive that, at times, the mainstream press appears to act as an extension of the CIA. As Carl Bernstein noted in a major investigation published in *Rolling Stone* magazine: "the sheer number of covert relationships with journalists was far greater than the CIA had ever hinted; and *the Agency's use of reporters and news executives was an intelligence asset of the first magnitude. Reporters had been involved in almost every conceivable kind of operation.*" [emphasis added] Carl Bernstein, "The CIA And The Media," *Rolling Stone*, October 20, 1977.

[306] Sarah Lyall, "British Press Uncovers Spy Scandal Of Its Own," *New York Times*, 12/20/98

[307] One of these studies was conducted by Carl Bernstein and published in *Rolling Stone Magazine* (Carl Bernstein, "The CIA And The Media," *Rolling Stone*, October 20, 1977). Another was written by John Crewdson and published on the front page of the *New York Times* on three consecutive days–December 25-27, 1977. The *Columbia Journalism Review* also published several investigations of CIA/media infiltration and cooperation. See: "The CIA, the FBI and the Media," *Columbia Journalism Review*, July/August, 1976, pp. 37-42 and Stuart H. Loory,

"The CIA's Use of the Press: a 'Mighty Wurlitzer'," *Columbia Journalism Review*, September/October, 1974, pp. 9-18.

[308] John M. Crewdson, "The C.I.A.'s 3-Decade Effort To Mold the World's Views: Agency Network Using News Organs, Books and Other Methods Is Detailed," *New York Times*, 12/25/77

[309] John L. Crewdson, "Worldwide Propaganda Network Built by the C.I.A.," *New York Times*, 12/26/77

[310] As was documented previously, the illegality of domestic covert actions was not necessarily a deterrent to CIA behavior.

[311] John Crewdson reported: "In the Times's study it appeared that the C.I.A. relied on its connections with Time, Newsweek, CBS News and The Times itself more extensively than on its contacts with other news organizations." [John M. Crewdson, "CIA: Secret Shaper Of Public Opinion: C.I.A. Established Many Links To Journalists in U.S. and Abroad," *New York Times*, 12/27/77] Carl Bernstein made similar observations writing that "according to Senate sources and CIA officials, an unavoidable conclusion emerged: that to a degree never widely suspected, the CIA in the 1950s, '60s and even early '70s had concentrated its relationships with journalists in the most prominent sectors of the American press corps, including four or five of the largest newspapers in the country, the broadcast networks and the two major newseekly magazines."

[312] As Kathryn Olmsted reported: "But even when a newspaper or network did not have a formal relationship with the CIA, the Agency could still have close ties and mutual interests with its reporters and editors." Kathryn Olmstead, "Challenging the Secret Government: Congress and the Press Investigate the Intelligence Community, 1974-1976," (Ph.D. diss., University of California, Davis, 1993), p. 32.

[313] As a recent editorial in the *New York Times* stated: "During the cold war, a pattern of informal collaboration developed between some journalists and the Central Intelligence Agency. Foreign correspondents and the C.I.A. station chiefs sometimes swapped information. In 1976, a Senate committee headed by Frank Church learned that this practice had gotten out of hand. Fifty journalists at various times had been paid by the C.I.A., and many more were used as "unwitting sources." "No Press Cards for Spies," *New York Times*, 3/18/96

[314] The *Columbia Journalism Review* described the situation as "the whole tangled web of relationships between reporters and intelligence agents."

[315] John M. Crewdson, "C.I.A. Established Many Links To Journalists in U.S. and Abroad," *New York Times*, 12/27/77

[316] Kathryn Olmstead, "Challenging the Secret Government: Congress and the Press Investigate the Intelligence Community, 1974-1976," (Ph.D. diss., University of California, Davis, 1993), p. 33.

[317] Kathryn Olmsted, "'*An American Conspiracy*': The Post-Watergate Press and the CIA," *Journalism History*, vol. 19, no. 2, 1993, p. 52.

[318] Ibid., p. 54.

[319] The *Columbia Journalism Review* summarized the situation in the following manner: "The open flow of personnel between the news business and the CIA is

known to many Washington journalists but is accepted and no particular point is made of it." Stuart H. Loory, "The CIA's Use of the Press: a 'Mighty Wurlitzer'," *Columbia Journalism Review*, September/October, 1974, p. 10.

[320] Chris Weinkopf, "William F. Buckley Jr.," *Salon.com*, Sept. 3, 1999.

[321] Given that Braden was intimately involved with the CIA's attempts to pre-empt the legitimate left with a manufactured Non-Communist Left, it is natural to wonder if Braden was himself playing a similar role—posing as a liberal media pundit, much like Oswald posed as a Marxist defender of Cuba in the media in New Orleans after he was exposed as a U.S. defector with Russian sympathies.

[322] Frances Stonor Saunders, *The Cultural Cold War: The CIA And The World of Arts and Letters*, (New York: The New Press, 1999), p. 95.

[323] John Crewdson, "Worldwide Propaganda Network Built by the C.I.A.," *New York Times*, 12/26/77

[324] Propaganda expert and MIT linguistics professor Noam Chomsky has summarized the utility of constraining debate within such manufactured bounds: "Any expert in indoctrination will confirm, no doubt, that it is far more effective to constrain all possible thought within a framework of tacit assumption than to try to impose a particular explicit belief with a bludgeon." And, specifically with respect to the establishment media: "the system has created the illusion of free and open debate while in fact ensuring that only a narrow spectrum of opinion and analysis reaches a broad public." Noam Chomsky, *Towards a New Cold War*, (New York: Pantheon Books, 1982), p. 81; Noam Chomsky, *Language and Politics*, (New York: Black Rose Books, 1988), p. 294.

[325] In 1967, Braden penned an article summarizing the extent of covert CIA manipulation in the *Saturday Evening Post*. In the article titled "I'm Glad the CIA is 'Immoral'", Braden wrote, "By 1953 we were operating or influencing international organizations in every field." Apparently very disillusioned, Braden, who had actively campaigned for the creation of the CIA, would later advocate its dissolution. Summarizing his views in a 1975 *Saturday Review* article he stated, "It's a shame what happened to the CIA. It could have consisted of a few hundred scholars to analyze intelligence, a few hundred spies in key positions, and a few hundred operators ready to carry out rare tasks of derring-do. Instead, it became a gargantuan monster, owning property all over the world, running airplanes and newspapers and radio stations and banks and armies and navies..." Saunders, pp. 95, 398, 423.

[326] Hinckle and Turner, p. 185.

[327] Frances Stonor Saunders, *The Cultural Cold War: The CIA And The World of Arts and Letters*, (New York: The New Press, 1999), pp. 146-7.

[328] As the *Washington Post* noted (with respect to the explosive issue of CIA-backed international assassinations) while covering the hearings: "The Rockefeller commission has decided to keep secret all of the evidence it has compiled about the Central Intelligence Agency's involvement in assassination plots, it was disclosed last night." When Nelson was accused by Frank Church of "playing down the CIA's misdeeds" during the investigation he responded (while holding a copy of the

report): "I don't think there is very much that hasn't been uncovered and discussed in this report..." George Lardner, Jr. "Rockefeller Unit to Keep Slaying Plot Data Secret," *Washington Post*, 6/6/75

[329] Gerard Colby, Charlotte Dennett, *Thy Will Be Done, The Conquest of the Amazon: Nelson Rockefeller and Evangelism in the Age of Oil*, (New York: HarperCollins Publishers, Inc., 1995), pp. 265-66.

[330] William Greider, Thomas O'Toole, "Rockefeller Family Holdings Touch Every Economic Sphere," *Washington Post*, 9/22/74

[331] James Bamford, *The Puzzle Palace: Inside the National Security Agency, America's Most Secret Intelligence Organization*, (New York: Penguin Books Ltd, 1986), pp. 119, 428-429.

[332] Stuart H. Loory, "The CIA's Use of the Press: a 'Mighty Wurlitzer'," *Columbia Journalism Review*, September/October, 1974, p. 9.

[333] Kathryn Olmstead, "Challenging the Secret Government: Congress and the Press Investigate the Intelligence Community, 1974-1976," (Ph.D. diss., University of California, Davis, 1993), p. 33.

[334] Kathryn Olmsted, "'An American Conspiracy': The Post-Watergate Press and the CIA," *Journalism History*, vol. 19, no. 2, 1993, p. 52.

[335] "No Press Cards for Spies," *New York Times*, 3/18/96

[336] Guatemala was used as a base for training many of the soldiers who fought in the Bay of Pigs invasion of Cuba. As Colby and Dennett summarized: "[M]any of the same CIA operatives that had overthrown the Arbenz government [of Guatemala] returned to Guatemala to begin preparations for another CIA invasion." (Colby and Dennett, p. 321.) According to many researchers it was the Bay of Pigs operation that made the Kennedy brothers suspicious of and hostile towards the CIA. Various operatives such as E. Howard Hunt and Frank Sturgis who were involved in these covert actions seem to reappear in investigations of the Kennedy assassination.

[337] In the mid 1960s, *Ramparts* magazine published an exposé of how the CIA used tax-exempt foundations to fund an international network of front groups. To discredit the story and its source, the CIA covertly attacked the magazine's publishers. As Saunders reported: "For more than a year the CIA did everything it could to sink *Ramparts*. 'I had all sorts of dirty tricks to hurt their circulation and financing,' Deputy Inspector General Edgar Applewhite later confessed. 'The people running *Ramparts* were vulnerable to blackmail. We had awful things in mind, some of which we carried off...We were not the least inhibited by the fact that the CIA had no internal security role in the United States.'" Saunders, p. 382.

[338] The CIA approached Random House and attempted to buy up all the copies of the book in advance. Random House offered to let the CIA buy up the first printing run but promised a second and third printing.

[339] John M. Crewdson, "The C.I.A.'s 3-Decade Effort To Mold the World's Views: Agency Network Using News Organs, Books and Other Methods Is Detailed," *New York Times*, 12/25/77

[340] As the *New York Times* reported: "But a C.I.A. document, recently declassified under the Freedom of Information Act, provides a detailed account of at least one

instance in which the agency mustered its propaganda machinery to support an issue of far more concern to Americans, and to the C.I.A. itself, than to citizens of other countries....This was the conclusion of the Warren Commission that Lee Harvey Oswald alone was responsible for the assassination of President Kennedy." "Cable Sought to Discredit Critics of Warren Report," *New York Times*, 12/26/77

[341] Alarmingly, this effort may have been a CIA-backed psychological warfare effort aimed at the American people. A similar "psywar" effort using the media was leveled against the people of Guatemala in the overthrow of the Arbenz government in 1954 and against the Cuban people as part of the Bay of Pigs invasion. There are links between personnel involved in these psywar operations against Cuba and Guatemala and personnel involved in the Kennedy assassination. For example, E. Howard Hunt, who was involved in both of these operations (and, it is alleged by some authors, the Kennedy assassination) was a member of Eisenhower's psychological warfare committee designed to facilitate the overthrow of the Guatemalan and Cuban governments. Hunt also headed up (as its first chief) the CIA's Domestic Operations Division–the very agency that participated in much of the covert action aimed at spying on American dissidents (which he claims actually began in 1962 under Kennedy). If Oswald was in fact working for the CIA or FBI as part of this domestic infiltration of anti-war groups, he may very well have been working for Hunt. Interestingly Hunt, as part of his service in the Domestic Ops Division, participated in, according to the *New York Times* "the secret financing of a Washington news agency." See: Lawrence C. Soley, "Radio Warfare: OSS and CIA Subversive Propaganda," (New York: Praeger, 1989), pp. 222-223; Seymour Hersh, "Hunt Tells of Early Work For a C.I.A. Domestic Unit," *New York Times*, 12/31/96

[342] "Conspiracy theories have frequently thrown suspicion on our organization, for example by falsely alleging that Lee Harvey Oswald worked for us. The aim of this dispatch is to provide material for countering and discrediting the claims of the conspiracy theorists, so as to inhibit circulation of such claims in other countries." Memo from CIA dated April 1, 1967 quoted in: "Cable Sought to Discredit Critics of Warren Report," *New York Times*, 12/26/77

[343] "These critics and others, the C.I.A. said, should be depicted as 'wedded to theories adopted before the evidence was in,' politically or financially 'interested' in disproving the commission's conclusion, 'hasty or inaccurate in their research, or infatuated with their own theories.'" "Cable Sought to Discredit Critics of Warren Report," *New York Times*, 12/26/77

[344] The *Times* reported: "Among the arguments that the agency suggested were that the Warren Commission had conducted 'as thorough an investigation as humanly possible, that the charges of the critics are without serious foundation, and that further speculative discussion only plays into the hands of the opposition.'"

[345] In light of this CIA memo that recommended the use of editorials and book reviews to further the Agency's propaganda goals, the near universal acclaim that Gerald Posner's CIA-favorable book *Case Closed* received from the establishment media organizations deserves closer attention. (The cover of *Newsweek Magazine* on Aug. 30- Sept. 6, 1993, sported the headlines: "CASE CLOSED: AFTER 30

YEARS OF CONSPIRACY THEORIES, A BRILLIANT NEW BOOK FINALLY PROVES WHO KILLED KENNEDY.") This favorable press should be compared with stunning silence with which John Newman's recent book *Oswald and the CIA* has been greeted by the same media outlets. Apparently, Newman made the mistake of actually bothering to read and report on the mountains of recently declassified documents that clearly show that the CIA has been less than forthcoming about its knowledge of Oswald's activities prior to the assassination.

[346] "The C.I.A. was careful to caution its stations overseas not to initiate a discussion 'of the assassination question' where such a discussion was 'not already taking place.' But where such discussions were under way, C.I.A. officers abroad were directed to 'discuss the publicity problem with liaison and friendly elite contacts, especially politicians and editors,' and to 'employ propaganda assets to answer and refute the attacks of the critics.'" "Cable Sought to Discredit Critics of Warren Report," *New York Times*, 12/26/77

[347] Final Report of the Senate Select Committee on Intelligence Activities, Excerpts reprinted in "The CIA, the FBI and the Media," *Columbia Journalism Review*, July/August, 1976, pp. 37-42.

[348] "The FBI has attempted covertly to influence the public's perception of persons and organizations by disseminating derogatory information to the press, either anonymously or through 'friendly' news contacts." Final Report of the Senate Select Committee on Intelligence Activities, Excerpts reprinted in "The CIA, the FBI and the Media," *Columbia Journalism Review*, July/August, 1976, p. 39.

[349] Final Report of the Senate Select Committee on Intelligence Activities, Excerpts reprinted in "The CIA, the FBI and the Media," *Columbia Journalism Review*, July/August, 1976, p. 42.

[350] "The bureau sometimes used its media contacts to prevent or postpone the publication of articles it considered favorable to its targets or unfavorable to the FBI. For example, to influence articles that related to the FBI, the bureau took advantage of a close relationship with a high official of a major national magazine, described in an FBI memorandum as 'our good friend.' Through this relationship, the FBI 'squelched' an 'unfavorable article against the Bureau' written by a free-lance writer about an FBI investigation; 'postponed publication' of an article on another FBI case; 'forestalled publication' of an article by Dr. Martin Luther King, Jr. and received information about proposed editing of King's articles." Final Report of the Senate Select Committee on Intelligence Activities, Excerpts reprinted in "The CIA, the FBI and the Media," *Columbia Journalism Review*, July/August, 1976, p. 41.

[351] Final Report of the Senate Select Committee on Intelligence Activities, Excerpts reprinted in "The CIA, the FBI and the Media," *Columbia Journalism Review*, July/August, 1976, p. 40.

[352] The ability of the CIA to censor the press has continued despite laws regulating CIA infiltration of the media (see below). As the *Boston Globe* reported as late as 1989: "William Baker, a former information officer...told a Harvard University audience that improved relations between the press and the CIA had helped him to

persuade three major newspapers or their reporters to kill, alter or delay articles concerning CIA operations." Stephen Kurkjian, Jeff McConnell, "Restraining the Media at the CIA," *Boston Globe*, 8/22/89

[353] In this case, editors were given a luncheon-briefing on CIA assassination plots by President Ford (a member of the Warren Commission) and asked not to write about it. They complied. Kathryn Olmsted, "'*An American Conspiracy*': The Post-Watergate Press and the CIA," *Journalism History*, vol. 19, no. 2 1993, pp. 51-58.

[354] One of the articles which got Hersh in trouble appeared on the front page of the *New York Times* in 1974: Seymour M. Hersh, "Huge C.I.A. Operation Reported In U.S. Against Antiwar Forces, Other Dissidents In Nixon Years," *New York Times*, 12/22/74

[355] Olmsted relates how the CIA brass intervened with the prestige-media's editors and owners to squelch impending stories relating to the CIA's embarrassing attempts to raise a sunken Soviet sub. Arguing that they would be exposing a potentially ongoing national security related operation, CIA management was able to convince many editors within the elite national press corps to self-censor the sub stories.

[356] The violent anti-Castro paramilitary operations of the CIA-backed group Alpha-66 were reported to be ongoing into the 1980s.

[357] There is another dimension to the media's lack of independence when it comes to reporting on covert activities. That dimension is the media's active participation in covert actions. In the case of the anti-Castro activities that are highly relevant to the Kennedy assassination, the actions of the media Goliath of Time-Life must be considered. This media giant was not an independent observer of the paramilitary activities against Castro's Cuba. The media outlet's owner, Henry Luce, used his publishing empire to directly aid these activities as well as to prepare the American people to support them. For example, Luce directed employees of Time, Inc. to provide logistical and financial assistance to the anti-Castro effort. *Life* purchased ship-to-shore radios for the commandos participating in the raids and provided insurance for both the commandos and the reporters covering the operations. The pages of *Life* magazine were also used to glamorize the commando raids against Cuba. (President Kennedy asked Luce to curtail these stories to avoid unwanted publicity of the ongoing paramilitary operations. Luce was reportedly greatly offended at this suggestion.) These considerations should make it apparent that the Time-Life media monolith would not exactly be a neutral institution reporting on the anti-Castro efforts or the Kennedy assassination since the corporation's owner took direct action in the anti-Castro efforts and was at odds with President Kennedy over coverage of the raids. [See: Hinckle and Turner, pp. 184-188.] Recall it was *Life* magazine which on February 21, 1964 published the famous and incriminating backyard photos of Oswald "proudly holding a Trotskyite newspaper, *The Militant*, in one hand and rifle he used to shoot President Kennedy in the other." The day after the assassination, *Life* purchased exclusive television and movie rights to the famous Zapruder film of the assassination and controlled publication of frames from the home-movie.

[358] According to the journal *Editor & Publisher*, it is a crime "to publish information about U.S. communications intelligence." *Editor & Publisher*, June 7, 1986, p. 13.
[359] Steve Komarow, "CIA Chief: Journalists Can Be Spies," *USA Today*, 2/23/96
[360] Gerald F. Seib, "Reporters, Spies and the Reasons They Don't Mix," *The Wall Street Journal*, 3/6/96
[361] Frank Smyth, "My Spy Story," *New York Times*, 2/22/96
[362] Ibid., 2/22/96
[363] Gerald F. Seib, "Reporters, Spies and the Reasons They Don't Mix," *The Wall Street Journal*, 3/6/96
[364] Steve Komarow, "CIA Chief: Journalists Can Be Spies," *USA Today*, 2/23/96
[365] To its credit, the *New York Times* did produce one editorial sharply criticizing renewed attempts to remove the barriers between the CIA and the media. The *Times* editorialized: "The prohibition on paying accredited journalists for intelligence work should be absolute. The same applies to issuing bogus press credentials to a covert agent." "No Press Cards for Spies," *New York Times*, 3/18/96
[366] Alan Saracevic, "All the News That's Safe to Print," *Mother Jones*, Jan./Feb. 1996, p. 14.
[367] As the *Times* summarized: "A decade ago, when the agency's communications empire was at its peak, it embraced more than 800 news and public information organizations and individuals." John Crewdson, "Worldwide Propaganda Network Built by the C.I.A.," *New York Times*, 12/26/77

Lightning Source UK Ltd.
Milton Keynes UK
UKOW050056181111

182228UK00002B/142/A